People's Republic of China

People's Republic of China

Revised Edition

BY KIM DRAMER

Enchantment of the World
Second Series

Children's Press®

A Division of Scholastic Inc.

NEW YORK   TORONTO   LONDON   AUCKLAND   SYDNEY
MEXICO CITY   NEW DELHI   HONG KONG
DANBURY, CONNECTICUT

Frontispiece: Women in a rice field near Ping'an

Consultant: Professor Nicole Huang, Department of East Asian Languages and Literature, University of Wisconsin-Madison.

Please note: All statistics are as up-to-date as possible at the time of publication.

Book production by Herman Adler Design

Library of Congress Cataloging-in-Publication Data

Dramer, Kim.
  People's Republic of China, revised edition / by Kim Dramer—Rev. ed.
      p. cm. — (Enchantment of the World. Second series)
  Audience: 10–14.
  Includes index.
  ISBN-10: 0-516-24867-7
  ISBN-13: 978-0-516-24867-7
  1. China—Juvenile literature. I. Title. II. Series.
  DS706.D73 2006
  951—dc22   2005024578

People's Republic of China

Contents

Cover photo:
Fishing on the
Li River

Farm fields

Han statue

The Center of the World

8

CHINA IS CONSIDERED THE WORLD'S OLDEST CONTINUOUS civilization. Over thousands of years, Chinese civilization has changed tremendously. But some of the most basic traditions that define China have changed little through the centuries. The Chinese still use an ancient writing system today, and the ideas of the ancient philosopher Confucius still form the basis of how human relations are viewed.

Opposite: **The Temple of Heaven is one of Beijing's most famous landmarks. It was completed in 1420, during the Ming dynasty.**

Trees grow atop towering Chinese peaks.

The first unified Chinese empire was formed in 221 B.C., when seven warring states were united by a conqueror from the state of Qin. He was called Shi Huangdi, which means "first emperor." All rulers of imperial China until the twentieth century called themselves the emperor.

The first emperor united China with a series of reforms and a massive building campaign. He standardized the weights and measures used in trade. He also standardized written Chinese characters so that people who spoke different dialects, or versions, of Chinese could still understand each other. That system of writing served as the basis of the writing system the Chinese use today. The written link between China's past and present is unique in the world.

Writing "China"

Chinese writing does not have an alphabet. Instead, it has symbols called characters, which represent words or parts of words. The Chinese characters for the word *China* reflect the Chinese people's view of their country's place in the world. The character on the left means "middle." The character on the right, "kingdom," shows the borders of the territory surrounding a spear that the Chinese used in their defense. This shows how the ancient Chinese thought of China as the center of the world, surrounded by weaker kingdoms. To this day, the Chinese call their country the Middle kingdom.

The first emperor built for himself a huge tomb guarded by thousands of clay soldiers. He also connected a series of ancient walls. These are thought to be the beginning of the Great Wall, a 2,500-mile-long (4,000-kilometer-long) wall built to protect China from invaders. The Great Wall is an enduring symbol of China.

The first Chinese emperor had a spectacular tomb built for himself. It includes more than seven thousand pottery soldiers, horses, and chariots.

Geopolitical map of China

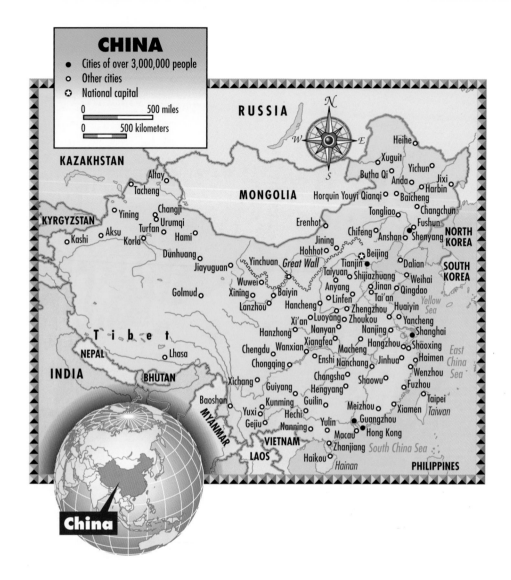

China was ruled by a series of dynasties—emperors belonging to the same family—after the Qin dynasty. The Chinese believed that each emperor ruled China through heaven's approval. This was called the "mandate of heaven," an agreement among the emperor, his subjects, and his heavenly ancestors. This system of rule ensured lengthy and relatively peaceful dynasties for more than two thousand years. During that period, Chinese people made many scientific and technological advances and achieved greatness in literature and the fine arts.

Today, China is the world's most populous nation, with more than a billion people. It is poised as an emerging world superpower. But it is also aware of its precious heritage and the value of its traditions. This link between China's past, present, and future can be seen in many of China's most technologically advanced ventures.

The Imperial Vault of Heaven is part of Beijing's Temple of Heaven complex. It once held important religious tablets.

One example of the link between sophisticated scientific efforts and China's traditions can be found in plans by the Chinese Academy of Sciences to launch a series of satellites to study the Moon. The first probe, which has a planned launch in 2007, will orbit the Moon for at least twelve months. It will perform such tasks as taking three-dimensional images of the Moon's surface, measuring the density of its soil, and analyzing its surface materials. The probe has been named *Chang'e 1*. This name links China's most sophisticated space technology with an ancient Chinese legend about a beautiful young woman named Chang'e.

China has been making great advances in space exploration in recent years. In 2005, the Chinese launched their second manned space mission.

According to the legend, Chang'e's husband, an archer named Yi, had a pill that gave immortality. Whoever swallowed the pill would never die. Yi hid the pill in the rafters of their house. Seeing a glow, his curious young wife discovered the pill and swallowed it. She knew that her husband would be angry with her. When she heard him return home, Chang'e opened the window to escape. She flew up to the Moon so quickly that Yi's arrows could not bring her down. The legend says that to this day, Chang'e lives in the palace of the Moon.

Past, present, and future come together in the *Chang'e 1* space probe. This is typical of the way that China's future will be built upon its rich cultural foundation.

This image from 1885 shows Chang'e fleeing to the moon.

A Land of Contrasts

CHINA IS A SPRAWLING COUNTRY. STRETCHING OVER much of east Asia, it is the world's third-largest nation; only Russia and Canada are larger. China can be divided into two huge areas: Inner China, which lies in the east and the south, and Outer China, which lies to the north and the west.

Opposite: **A camel caravan travels across the sand dunes in Gansu Province.**

Inner China

Inner China is a low-lying area of fertile land. The region is home to China's most productive farmland. Much of Inner China is hilly. It is densely populated and crisscrossed by a complex network of transportation routes. Roads, railways, and water routes link the Yangtze River and the Yellow River with the eastern coast.

Farmers tend fertile fields in the valleys between some of China's steep mountain slopes.

Inner China can be divided into north and south. The north is dominated by the Yellow River. The south is dominated by the Yangtze River. The Yellow River gets its name from the yellow silt in its waters. This silt, called loess, is very fine sand, blown by the winds from the Gobi Desert in the west. Over thousands of years, deposits of loess that are hundreds of feet deep have accumulated over the central plain of northern China. As the Yellow River cuts through this layer of loess, its waters become yellow.

The Yellow River meanders for 2,920 miles (4,700 km) across northern China. It is the nation's second-longest river.

The Yellow River is so prone to flooding that it has earned the name China's Sorrow. Over the centuries, the Chinese have built dikes to control the waters. The dikes are so high in certain sections that the water actually flows above the lands that border it.

The waters of the Yangtze River are more stable. The Yangtze's water flow is regulated by two great lakes in its middle course—the Dongting and the Poyang. These lakes act as natural reservoirs in times of drought. They also provide overflow basins to prevent flooding.

The Yangtze is the longest river in Asia and the third-longest in the world. One-third of China's people live in the Yangtze River valley.

The Three Gorges Dam

The Three Gorges have long been considered one of China's scenic wonders. These towering limestone cliffs form a 200-mile (300 km) canyon along the Yangtze River. But China is building the world's largest dam on the Yangtze, and the lake behind that dam will flood the Three Gorges, changing its beauty forever.

Building the Three Gorges Dam has been called China's most ambitious project since the Great Wall. It is designed to control flooding and produce hydroelectric power.

Many people criticize the project, however. The Chinese government has had to resettle more than a million people living along the banks of the Yangtze because their land will be flooded. Valuable ancient sites will also be flooded. Other experts cite the environmental damage caused by the

dam. Despite the complaints, the project is under way, and it began generating power in 2003. The dam is scheduled to be completed in 2009.

The Grand Canal

Over the centuries, the Chinese built a series of canals to link the Yellow River in the north to the Yangtze River in the south. The most important part of this system is the Grand Canal.

The Grand Canal begins in Beijing and ends in Hangzhou. It links the Hai, Yellow, Yangtze, and Qiantang rivers. The Grand Canal is the oldest and longest human-made waterway in the world. The 1,114-mile-long (1,795-km-long) canal took 1,769 years to build—from 486 B.C. to A.D. 1283. It stands as a magnificent achievement of ancient China.

During times of famine, the Grand Canal was the lifeline that brought grain from the south to starving people in the north. The canal also made it easier to collect taxes and transport soldiers. Before parts of it silted up over the last century, the Grand Canal provided irrigation to surrounding farmers. It also helped develop economic and cultural ties between northern and southern China.

China's Geographic Features

Area: 3,705,820 square miles (9,598,032 sq km)

Largest City: Shanghai, 17,420,000 people

Highest Elevation: Mount Everest (Qomolangma), 29,028 feet (8,848 m)

Lowest Elevation: Turpan Depression, 505 feet (154 m) below sea level

Longest River: Yangtze (Chang), 3,434 miles (5,429 km)

Largest Desert: Gobi Desert, 500,000 square miles (1,295,000 sq km)

Highest Average Precipitation: 80 inches (200 cm) on the southeastern coast

Lowest Average Precipitation: Less than 4 inches (11 cm) in the northern deserts

The Great Wall

The Great Wall marks the traditional border between Inner and Outer China. The main part of the wall is about 2,500 miles (4,000 km) long. Some sections of the wall rise as high as 35 feet (11 meters).

Ancient Chinese people began building long walls in the third century B.C. to protect against invaders. Few traces of these earthen walls remain. Most of what is today called the Great Wall was built during the Ming dynasty in the late fifteenth century.

When the Great Wall was being constructed more than two thousand years ago, the emperor used war prisoners and criminals as laborers. But when the work proved too slow, he ordered Chinese farmers to leave their fields and help complete the project. The workers often went hungry and toiled in the bitter winter without warm clothing. When a worker died, the body was often thrown into the rubble and covered with bricks. The Great Wall thus became a symbol of oppression and cruelty as well as of the might of the emperor.

For most Chinese people, the Great Wall is a source of pride and an important part of China's identity. It is a symbol of the nation's civilization and patriotism. The Chinese point to the work of the ordinary men and women who labored to build the wall. They also see the Great Wall as a symbol of China's historic military strength.

Outer China

Outer China is an area of physical extremes and spectacular scenery. It is home to the world's highest mountain, Everest (Qomolangma), some 29,028 feet (8,848 m) above sea level. In the southwest, the Himalaya, a towering mountain range, rise from a great plateau. The soaring peaks are covered with ice, while the plateau below is dry, rocky, and unsuitable for farming. This region of China is called the Plateau of Tibet.

Mount Everest is the highest peak on Earth. In 1953, New Zealander Edmund Hillary and Nepalese Tenzing Norgay became the first people to climb all the way to its summit.

Qomolangma

The highest point on Earth, majestic Qomolangma (Mount Everest) rises on the border of Nepal and Tibet in China. Local people call it the Goddess Mother of the World. The mountain's English name honors Sir George Everest, a British official in India in the 1800s.

At the top of Qomolangma, oxygen levels are low, temperatures are cold, and winds are powerful. Because of these extremes, the mountain peak has no plant or animal life. People first climbed to the peak of the mountain in 1953.

Northwestern China is blanketed by huge deserts, including the Ordos, the Gobi, and the Taklimakan. China's lowest point is also located in this region. The Turpan Depression dips 505 feet (154 m) below sea level. But the northwest also has towering mountains, the Tian Shan range, with peaks rising to over 20,000 feet (6,000 m).

The barren Turpan Depression receives almost no rain.

Historically, Outer China was cut off from Inner China by dangerous terrain and impassable areas. The famous Silk Routes were a complex network of trade routes linking China to the Middle East, Europe, and India. Over the centuries, both trade goods and ideas traveled along the Silk Routes. China's silk, tea, and porcelains were transported by camel caravan. Traders brought ideas such as the religion of Buddhism along the routes with them. These new ideas made their way into the culture of Inner China.

Inner and Outer China are about the same size, but Outer China is home to only 5 percent of the country's population. Outer China's frontier areas are the homeland of many of China's ethnic minorities.

Huge statues honoring the Silk Routes stand in Xi'an. The Silk Route connecting China to the West was first used in the second century B.C.

The Coastline

China has a long coastline that stretches from the Yalu River in the north to the Beilun River on the China-Vietnam border in the south. The Chinese mainland borders three seas that are part of the Pacific Ocean—the Yellow Sea, the East China Sea, and the South China Sea.

China has more than five thousand coastal islands. The vast majority of these islands are scattered in the coastal waters south of Hangzhou Bay and the South China Sea. The largest of these islands is Taiwan. Although China claims Taiwan, it has been governed independently since 1949. The largest island under China's rule is Hainan Island in the South China Sea. Products such as coconuts and tea are grown on Hainan. This island is also home to a major submarine base.

People fish from the rocks on one of China's thousands of islands.

Climate

Because China is spread out over such an immense area and has such a varied landscape, its weather includes extremes from bitter cold to unbearable heat. China's climate follows a general pattern of change, from tropical in the southeast through a cooler middle belt, ending in arid and high-mountain climates in the northwest. The hottest spot in China is Turpan, located in the north. Temperatures in summer may soar to 116 degrees Fahrenheit (47 degrees Celsius) but can drop to –22°F (–30°C) in winter.

Looking at China's Cities

Shanghai (below) is China's largest city. The name *Shanghai* means "upon the sea." Shanghai is located on the Huanpu River, where it empties into the East China Sea. During the nineteenth century, Shanghai was a major trading port for foreign powers. It retains its European flavor and its important place in international commerce. Today, the city is a global center for banking, shipping, and trade. Shanghai is striving to become the world's leading shipbuilding center.

Guangzhou (above), southern China's major port and city, was founded by the first Qin emperor in 214 B.C. Until 1842, it was the only Chinese port open to foreign trade.

Shenyang, in northeastern China, was founded in about A.D. 1000. It served as the Manchu capital until 1644. Today, Shenyang is a major industrial city, producing machinery, aircraft, and rubber goods. The city's residents have Manchu, Han Chinese, Korean, and Russian ancestors.

Tianjin is a major northern port and industrial city. High-quality bicycles and watches made in Tianjin are sold throughout China.

A Land of Contrasts **27**

Wild Things

28

CHINA IS AN ENORMOUS COUNTRY AND IS HOME TO A vast number of plants and animals. Antelope, wolves, bears, and deer are found across the nation. But other creatures are much less common. Some of the world's rarest deer, wild horses, mountain sheep, and wild cats live in the harsh terrain of Outer China. The endangered Chinese alligator is found only in the lower Yangtze River. Fewer than two hundred remain in the wild. Siberian tigers are also critically endangered in China, with fewer than 150 living in the wild.

Opposite: **Bactrian camels have two humps and stand more than 7 feet (2 m) tall. They were used by travelers on the Silk Routes.**

The Siberian tiger is the world's largest cat. It can eat 100 pounds (45 kilograms) at a single meal.

The giant panda is the animal most people associate with China. Called bear-cats by the Chinese, pandas have been around for 3 million years. Only about 1,600 giant pandas live in the wild. Most of the pandas are found in nature preserves in mountains near the Yangtze River. The forests there can support the pandas' limited diet. The creatures feed almost entirely on bamboo. If the pandas do not have enough bamboo, they cannot survive.

The pandas' diet is just one factor threatening their future. The creatures are also in danger because farming and development are taking over their habitat, forcing the pandas into a smaller area.

Giant pandas spend up to fourteen hours a day eating.

Animal Good Luck Symbols

The Chinese use many animals to symbolize good fortune. A flying dragon in the *I Ching*, an ancient Chinese book of wisdom, symbolizes that all under heaven is going well. Bats are a symbol of good luck because their name, *bien fu*, sounds the same as the word for "good luck." Likewise, fish (*yu*), whose name sounds the same as the word for "plentiful," are often depicted on dishes to express the wish for bounty. The *qilin* is a mythical animal that supposedly appears every five hundred years. Its birth signals the birth of a wise person such as the philosopher Confucius.

Relict Species

The panda is just one example of so-called relict species of plants and animals in China. Relict species are those that survived the Ice Age, a time when many other species became extinct. The dawn redwood, the only living relative of the California redwoods, is the most famous relict plant in China.

The ginkgo tree is another relict plant native to China. The hardy ginkgo is often planted in North American cities because it can withstand urban pollution. The ginkgo grows up to 100 feet (30 m) tall with a trunk 3 feet (1 m) in diameter. It has fan-shaped leaves and a plumlike fruit with thin, pulpy flesh and a large white seed. The fruit gives off a foul odor as it rots. The Chinese harvest the seeds for eating. One Chinese dessert is a dish of ginkgo seeds in burnt sugar sauce.

Gingko trees have delicate fan-shaped leaves.

Three Friends of Winter

Chinese people have found rich symbolism in the plants of the country to express their ideals and hopes. Most famous among these plants are the Three Friends of Winter— bamboo, plum blossom, and pine.

The bamboo is treasured for its ability to bend with the wind yet remain upright and straight. Its hollow stem is thought to be free of prejudice and judgment. For this reason, it symbolizes strength and everlasting friendship. The winter plum blossom symbolizes personal renewal. It is the first flower to blossom each spring. The pine tree's ability to withstand the rigors of frost symbolizes inner strength and longevity.

The Three Friends of Winter have come to symbolize the qualities needed in the face of hardship. They are often painted together in Chinese art. What may appear to be a charming landscape to a Westerner, then, is actually a moral statement about how to live life.

Plant Life

China is also home to many wild species of commonly cultivated plants, such as oranges, chestnuts, rice, and walnuts. Many flowers, trees, and fruits seen in North America originated in China. The orange, the rhododendron, the tea rose, and kiwifruit all came from China.

The lacquer, or varnish, tree is found near the Yellow River. The sap of lacquer trees is known for its strong adhesive quality and beautiful gloss. This sap is called lacquer. Thousands of years ago, the Chinese learned how to use lacquer to decorate objects. Lacquerware is made by brushing layers of the lacquer onto an object, often carved of wood. As the layers are built up, the object takes on a smooth, brilliant finish. The lacquer may be carved, gilded, or painted.

A woman removes silkworm larvae from their cocoons. It takes an estimated 2,500 to 3,000 cocoons to make one yard of silk fabric.

Silk

The manufacture of silk has been a hallmark of Chinese civilization for five thousand years. Silk manufacture depends on the combination of an animal and a plant—the silkworm and the mulberry tree. The silkworm feeds solely on mulberry leaves. Each spring, these leaves are harvested to feed silkworms raised in captivity.

The silkworms spin a cocoon from a single strand of silk that is between 2,000 and 3,000 feet (600 and 900 m) long. These cocoons are soaked, steamed, and unwound to recover the silk strand. Several strands of silk are then combined to make a thread.

Silk making was a jealously guarded secret for centuries. One legend says that the secret of silk making was smuggled out of China by a princess. Commanded to marry a foreign prince in the West, she hid silk cocoons in an elaborate head-dress she wore as she left China for her new home.

Domestic Animals

The Silk Routes that crossed long stretches of desert relied on the two-humped Bactrian camel. These camels carried travelers and heavy loads among China, central Asia, India, and Europe. The camels' ability to run over desert sands made them valuable. They could also sniff out underwater springs and predict deadly sandstorms.

Many kinds of dog breeds began in China. The Pekingese used to be known as "sleeve dogs" because the tiny, short-legged breed could be carried in the long, flowing sleeves of wealthy Chinese. The shih tzu, developed in Beijing during the 1600s, was a great favorite of the emperors of China.

Working dogs from China include the chow chow and the shar-pei. The chow chow has been popular in China for at least two thousand years. It is big enough to be used as a guard dog and strong enough to pull carts. The

Shar-pei puppies have wrinkles all over their bodies. By the time they are full grown, however, the wrinkles are often limited to the head, neck, and shoulders.

shar-pei is known for the folds of loose skin covering its body, especially its head. It was developed for dogfighting, a popular sport in the 1500s, because the loose skin prevented other dogs from pinning it down.

Tibetan Animals

The geographic isolation of Tibet led to the breeding of distinctive types of dogs. The Tibetan spaniel was a companion of Buddhist monks in the monasteries of Tibet. The Lhasa apso is another dog associated with Tibetan Buddhism. The present of a Lhasa apso was a traditional gift of the Dalai Lama, a

The Lhasa apso is a small, muscular dog that is well adapted to Tibet's harsh climate. The Lhasa apso's coat keeps it warm during the long winters, and its long hair keeps the fierce wind out of its eyes.

Tiny Pets

Many Chinese children keep a cricket in a tiny cage as a summer pet. In the warm evenings, children fall asleep to the soothing sound of the cricket's chirping.

Another summer pet enjoyed by Chinese children is the cicada. As the summer sun sets, the shrill song of the cicada fills the air. This sound is produced by the vibrating skin on the abdomen of the male cicada. The cicada lives high up in the trees. To catch a cicada, Chinese children use a long bamboo pole with glue on one end.

The cicada has an unusually long cycle of life and death. It buries itself in the ground and emerges many years later, leaving a dried skin. Because of this cycle of life and death, the cicada was a symbol of rebirth to the ancient Chinese. Cicadas are common in Chinese art made for funerals.

Tibetan spiritual leader. The Tibetan mastiff is a large dog that can weigh up to 180 pounds (80 kilograms). It was originally bred for guarding flocks in the mountains of Tibet.

Tibet is home to many people who live a seminomadic, or wandering, life. They live in large tents called yurts and

Tibetans herd yaks in the shadow of Mount Kailish. There are about twelve million yaks in China.

survive by raising goats, sheep, and yaks. Hardy yaks are an important part of Tibetan life and culture. The yak has curved horns, short legs, high shoulders, and long hair hanging from its flanks, legs, and tail.

For Tibetans, the yak provides many of life's essentials. The hair of the yak is sheared and pounded together to make a felt cloth. This cloth is used to make tents that are naturally waterproof. The meat of the yak is eaten fresh or dried to make meat jerky. The milk of the yak is good to drink. Sometimes it is salted and added to tea. Yak milk is also churned into butter. Some of this butter is eaten, some is burned in lamps, and some is carved into sculptures. The Ta'er Lamasery, built in 1560, has a collection of yak butter sculpture depicting humans, animals, and landscapes. The art of butter sculpture probably dates back 1,300 years.

Yaks are also used to carry people and heavy loads. When a Tibetan family moves, it packs its yak-felt tent onto the back of a yak. During the move, the family will eat yak jerky and drink tea with yak milk and salt.

Yaks are native to the frigid high grasslands of Tibet. They can survive cold winter temperatures as low as -40°F (-40°C).

The March of History

EOPLE HAVE BEEN LIVING IN WHAT IS NOW CHINA FOR perhaps 500,000 years. These prehistoric people lived in caves in northern China. A number of distinct groups emerged by 10,000 B.C. Chinese civilization developed from two of these groups, the Yangshao and the Longshan. The Longshan people built walls around their settlements, grew rice, and raised sheep and cattle. Chinese history would come to be defined by dynasties, and the first Chinese dynasty—the Shang—developed out of the Longshan culture in the 1700s B.C.

Opposite: **This stone sculpture dates back to the Tang dynasty (618-907).**

Many axeheads and other objects made by the Shang and Longshan cultures have been discovered.

The Shang were led by a series of kings. Power passed down through a family. The king consulted his dead ancestors before making decisions. He would ask the spirits a question and then touch heated millet stalks to shells or bones until they cracked. The cracks were read to understand the answer of the spirits. The first Chinese writing developed during the Shang dynasty. This period also saw advances in music, science, metalwork, and stonework.

Jade

Ancient sites from China's stone age are marked by the presence of jade, an extremely hard stone. At first, jade was used only for ritual and political ornaments. Over time, it was used for personal adornment. Today, many Chinese wear a piece of jade. This is because jade came to be seen as possessing moral qualities. A dictionary from the Han period (206 B.C.–A.D. 220) describes jade this way:

> Jade is the fairest of stones. It is endowed with five virtues. **Charity** is typified by its luster, bright yet warm; **rectitude** by its translucency, revealing the color and markings within; **wisdom** by the purity and penetrating quality of its note when the stone is struck; **courage**, in that it may be broken, but cannot be bent; **equity**, in that it has sharp angles, which yet injure none.

Early Dynasties

The Shang were defeated by the Zhou, who had China's longest dynasty, ruling for almost a thousand years. The great philosopher Confucius (551–479 B.C.) lived during the Zhou dynasty. He developed a philosophy that would come to regulate society. Confucianism is based on the belief that man is basically good. The role of government is to maintain an orderly network of human relations and behavior. Confucius believed that a more perfect society could be formed when rulers and subjects, nobles and peasants, and all family members devoted themselves to their responsibilities to others.

During the Zhou period, there was constant warfare among the leaders of semi-independent regions. Confucius traveled to each court in turn, hoping to end the warfare. He tried to convince each lord to rule with the welfare of the people in mind rather than just being concerned with expanding their kingdoms. But he was unsuccessful.

China was united as a single, great empire when the lord of Qin subdued his rival feudal lords. He took the title of emperor, which was also used by the ruler of all later Chinese dynasties. The first Qin emperor, a warrior, disapproved of the philosophy of Confucius. Instead, he favored a strict policy of law and order. He ordered that all written records of Confucius's teachings be destroyed. At the same time, the first Qin emperor began a series of great public works aimed at unifying the Chinese empire. These included the linking of defensive walls and the construction of canals and roads. The Qin dynasty was short-lived. It ended in 206 B.C., just three years after the first emperor's death.

The first Qin emperor ordered that Confucian books be burned and scholars be killed.

Under the next dynasty, the Han, many of the hallmarks of Chinese imperial rule were established. Most important among these was the imperial examination system. This system awarded government jobs based on merit rather than on family status. The imperial exams, which helped make China's government more efficient, were given until the early 1900s.

Following the Han, the empire broke up into smaller kingdoms. Invasions by northern peoples became common. This period saw many foreign influences, including the spread of the Buddhist religion across China.

The empire was reunified when the Sui dynasty (A.D. 581–617) took control and linked north and south China by building the Grand Canal. This link between the Yangtze and the Yellow rivers allowed better communications and trade. The ability to transport grain from the south to the north allowed an army to be based at the northern border to defend the empire.

The art of the Han dynasty is noted for its small statues of horses and other figures.

A Golden Age

The Tang dynasty (618–907) was a golden age for Chinese culture. During this time, Chinese poetry, art, and trade flourished. The empire also expanded to the west and north.

Upheaval followed the end of the Tang dynasty, but the country was united once again under the Song dynasty (960–1279). The Song emperors were great patrons of the arts. Painting, calligraphy, and poetry became hallmarks of the Chinese elite.

More than a hundred thousand Buddhas have been sculpted in cliffs and caves across China. Buddhism entered China with traders traveling along the Silk Routes.

The threat of nomadic peoples in the north had long been a concern to China. One group, the Mongols, under the leadership of Kublai Khan, defeated the Song and established the Yuan dynasty in 1279. During the Yuan dynasty, which lasted until 1368, international trade along the Silk Routes thrived. In the West, China's reputation for luxury goods is said to have inspired the Venetian traveler Marco Polo to visit China. The Yuan established the Chinese capital at Beijing.

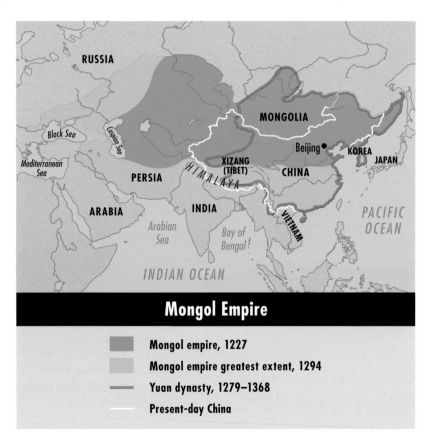

Mongol Empire

■ Mongol empire, 1227
■ Mongol empire greatest extent, 1294
— Yuan dynasty, 1279–1368
— Present-day China

The Mongols were driven from power by the Ming (1368–1644). During the Ming dynasty, the capital at Beijing was expanded, China's production of luxury goods flourished, and trade reached the east coast of Africa.

China's last dynasty, the Qing, was founded in 1644 by Manchu people from the north of China. The Qing dynasty would rule China until 1911. The middle part of the Qing dynasty was marked by able rulers and the expansion of the Chinese empire to its greatest limits, including Mongolia and Tibet.

The late Qing dynasty was noted for its conservative thinking and inward-looking isolationism. The West, meanwhile, was experiencing a flurry of technological and scientific advancement that China could not match. When foreign powers reached China's shores, the Qing emperors were unable to respond as military equals.

Foreign Influence

During the Qing dynasty, Europeans, Japanese, and Americans arrived at China's coast, demanding to become trading partners. They wanted China's silk, tea, and spices, but the Chinese were not purchasing much in return. Some European traders began bringing a drug called opium to China.

In this eighteenth-century scroll, Khirghiz people from central Asia present tribute horses to a Qing emperor. This was painted by Guiseppe Castiglione, an Italian who took the name Lang Shining while in China.

Importing opium into China was banned in 1796. But foreign powers ignored the order and continued to sell the moneymaking drug. Enraged, the Chinese seized 20,000 chests of British opium brought to Guangzhou in 1839. The British responded by attacking and defeating Chinese forces. This was the first of four Opium Wars. Each war ended with a humiliating treaty for China and the establishment of seaports to receive foreign goods. Soon a string of treaty ports stretched across China. These ports were home to foreign politicians and traders. They built Western-style homes, churches, and schools in areas where Chinese were forbidden to live. The Chinese became second-class citizens in their own country.

British soldiers go ashore during the First Opium War. Britain defeated China in the First Opium War in 1842.

Rebellions

Many Chinese found these conditions intolerable. In Guangzhou, the Taiping movement began. It called for public ownership of farms, fairer taxes, and the banning of slavery. The Qing government saw these calls for reform as a threat. In 1864, the Qing and foreigners—who preferred to deal with the weakened Qing government—fought together to defeat the Taiping.

The foreigners soon carved up China into "spheres of influence." By 1898, Russia, Germany, Britain, Japan, and France all claimed a piece of China. But the United States proposed an "open door" policy, leaving China open to trade with any foreign power. China was at the mercy of foreigners. The Chinese people demanded a change.

A new set of rebels, called the Boxers, now emerged. The Qing throne saw the Boxers as useful in ridding the country of foreigners, and the two Chinese factions eventually united. A massacre of foreigners and Chinese Christians began. In 1900, the foreigners' compound in Beijing was attacked.

Western powers responded by again defeating the Chinese. China became a nation in name only. A number of revolutionary groups began working to end the dynasty and establish a republic. In 1911, they did just that.

The Boxers were opposed to all foreign influences, including foreign religion. Thousands of Christians were killed during the Boxer Rebellion.

Sun Yat-sen

Sun Yat-sen, the father of the first Republic of China, was a medical doctor who had been educated in Japan. Sun's efforts to establish a Chinese republic received the support of educated Chinese as well as overseas Chinese who helped finance his efforts.

Sun's republic was based on his Three Principles of the People: nationalism, democracy, and the welfare of the people.

The Chinese Republic

The leader of these revolutionary groups, Sun Yat-sen, wished to found a new China on the ideas of democracy. Sun was proclaimed president of the Chinese Republic in 1912. Although there was a national capital in Beijing, much power lay in the hands of regional warlords.

In World War I (1914–1918), China entered on the Allied side, fighting with Britain, France, and the United States in their war against Germany. China sent workers to France, where manpower was critically short. Yet the Treaty of Versailles, which ended the war, ignored China. The defeated Germans were told to transfer their Chinese treaty ports to the Japanese instead of returning them to China.

Many Chinese were outraged. On May 4, 1919, thousands of students in Beijing took to the streets in a great political protest marked by violence and arrests. More protests followed.

In the end, China never signed the Treaty of Versailles. The government in Beijing backed down, and the arrested students were released. Public support for the students continued to grow. This became known as the May Fourth Movement.

The strong Chinese nationalism of the May Fourth Movement affected China's future political struggles. Young people rejected many elements of China's traditional culture. They rejected Confucianism in favor of increased social action, such as organizing labor unions.

Meanwhile, the Chinese Republic existed in name only. Sun did not have the power to rule. The power was in the hands of those who controlled the military. Struggles among military factions led by warlords made the nation unstable.

Many stores shut down in sympathy with the May Fourth Movement. Here, workers gather to listen to a student speak about the movement.

New Political Parties

China's intellectuals sought a new solution in Communism. The Communists believed that the government should control the economy. At Beijing University, a young librarian named Mao Zedong helped with the new Chinese Communist Party.

At the same time, the Kuomintang, or Nationalist Party, which had arisen after the end of the Qing dynasty, began to train its National Revolutionary Army. This army was led by Chiang Kai-shek. His plans for China were based on traditional rule by a small group. Chiang and Mao, each with a different view for China's future, were both trying to unite and modernize China while getting rid of foreign aggressors.

Chiang was appointed commander-in-chief of the National Revolutionary Army by both the Kuomintang and the

Mao Zedong

Mao Zedong grew up in a peasant family. He saw the unequal distribution of wealth and resources in China. The hardworking peasants farmed the land and lived in poverty, while the landlords owned large tracts of land and had great wealth. Mao Zedong's dream for China was a Communist government based on the ideas that everyone works together for the good of all the people and that all people are equal. Mao would go on to lead China for twenty-seven years.

The Changing Role of Women

In traditional China, the role of women was defined by the Three Confucian Obediences: to the father before marriage, to the husband after marriage, and to sons in widowhood. The lives of most Chinese women were spent within the family.

During the early 1900s, Chinese intellectuals began to question many Confucian values. Instead, they favored freedom and equality for men and women.

As China's political struggles intensified, many Chinese came to believe that the low status of women and the narrow scope of their activities were among the causes of national weakness and poverty. Freeing women was seen as a necessary part of the liberation of China. Many women took part in the May Fourth Movement and in the years of struggle between the Communists and the Nationalists.

Under Mao's Communist government, established with the founding of the People's Republic of China in 1949, Chinese women assumed, in theory, an equal status with men. To build a new China, women were asked to replace their traditional dedication to the family with self-sacrifice for the nation.

Communists. Troops began an effort to take power away from warlords in northern China and to fight the Japanese who had invaded China.

Civil War

It soon became clear that the Kuomintang and the Communists could not work together. A civil war began for control of the country in 1946. Poorly equipped and small in number, the Communists adopted the strategy of guerrilla warfare, irregular fighting by small groups. Their strategy was summed up in a slogan:

The enemy advances, we retreat;
The enemy camps, we harass;
The enemy tires, we attack;
The enemy retreats, we pursue.

The Long March

When Chiang's troops hemmed in 100,000 Communist troops in southern China, the Communists began a retreat to the north. They marched across some of the world's harshest terrain. This legendary Communist retreat, called the Long March, took an entire year and covered some 6,000 miles (10,000 km).

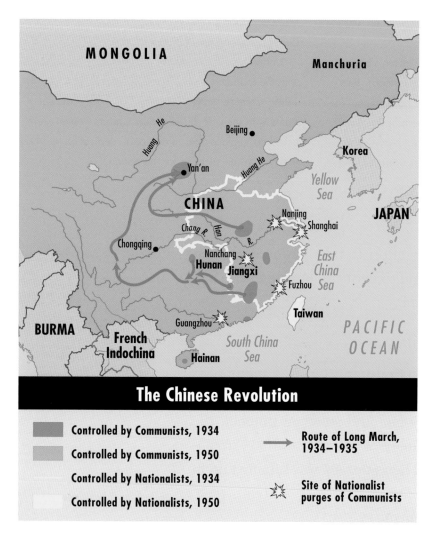

The Chinese Revolution

- Controlled by Communists, 1934
- Controlled by Communists, 1950
- Controlled by Nationalists, 1934
- Controlled by Nationalists, 1950
- → Route of Long March, 1934–1935
- ✦ Site of Nationalist purges of Communists

As the Communists trekked through China's remote and poor areas, they took lands away from wealthy landlords and gave them to poor peasants. Many of these peasants joined the Communist troops. They were issued guns that had been captured from the Nationalists. But sickness and fatigue took a terrible toll on the Communist troops. Only 20,000 men and women completed the Long March. Mao Zedong was among the survivors.

Mao Zedong (left) and thousands of other Communists fled Nationalist troops during the Long March.

The Long March proved that China's peasants would fight for Communism if they were given guns and hope. The power base for the Communists was not the educated class living in China's cities. It was the farming peasants.

World War II

Japan had been grabbing more and more Chinese territory throughout the 1930s. When the Japanese bombed the American naval base at Pearl Harbor, Hawaii, in 1941, China entered World War II on the side of the Allies. This group, which included the United States, Great Britain, and Russia, was fighting the Axis Powers, primarily Germany, Italy, and Japan. Japan was defeated in 1945. In China, the Communists and the Nationalists began their final battle for control.

Nationalist troops occupied China's major cities. The Communist troops had their power bases in the countryside. Now Nationalist troops found themselves outnumbered and surrounded by Communist forces. Thousands of Chiang's troops switched sides and joined the Communists in their fight for a new China.

The city of Nanjing, the Nationalist capital, fell to the Communists in April 1949 when Communist troops crossed the Yangtze River in a fleet of small fishing boats. The Nationalists fled as the Communists took all the major cities south of the Yangtze. In 1949, more than 2 million Nationalists followed Chiang Kai-shek to the island of Taiwan, off China's eastern coast. There they continued the government of the

Chiang Kai-shek struggled against the Communists for more than twenty years before finally fleeing to Taiwan in 1949. He served as president of Taiwan until his death in 1975.

Republic of China, refusing to submit to the Communist regime. Until his death in 1975, Chiang planned to return to mainland China and reclaim it.

On October 1, 1949, Mao Zedong, now chairman of the Chinese Communist Party, proclaimed the founding of the People's Republic of China. Mao proclaimed a new China based upon the fair distribution of land and goods and the equality of all of China's people.

The Cultural Revolution

The government took control of important industries and redistributed land. But China's farms were not producing enough food for its people. By 1966, Mao's economic policies had led to famine. To retain his political power, Mao designed an attack on his political opponents in the Chinese Communist Party and government. This became the Cultural Revolution.

Tens of thousands of young Chinese joined a militaristic group called the Red Guards. The Red Guards attacked the Communist Party bureaucracy. They claimed to be rooting out the evils of the elite in Chinese society. Included in the attacks were intellectuals, teachers, scientists, and politicians. These people were sent to the countryside for "reeducation" through hard labor. During the Cultural Revolution, monuments and temples were destroyed and religious worship was forbidden. There was chaos throughout the country. In 1969, Mao declared the Cultural Revolution over, and things slowly returned to normal.

New Flags

The design of the new Hong Kong flag shows a stylized five-petaled bauhinia flower, a native plant of Hong Kong, on a red background. In each petal is a star. This new flag thus links Hong Kong with the motherland by recalling the five stars on a red background in the flag of the People's Republic of China. It was adopted in 1997.

In 1999, Macau adopted a new flag as a symbol of reunification. It has a light green field with a white lotus above a stylized bridge and water. Above the flower is an arc of five stars, one large and four small as on the flag of China.

Leadership for the Future

Mao Zedong died in 1976, and Deng Xiaoping became the leader of China. He instituted policies of moderation and modernization. Deng, a Communist revolutionary, had played a major role in the civil war that led to the founding of the People's Republic of China. Deng's death in 1997 brought an end to the era of government by people who had fought alongside Mao in the revolution. The nation's new leader was Jiang Zemin, an engineer by training and the former mayor of Shanghai.

In 1989, Tiananmen Square, a large plaza in the middle of Beijing, became the focal point of Chinese politics. Students were protesting the corruption of Communist officials. They were also calling for democracy and greater equality among Chinese people. After weeks of demonstrations, thousands of soldiers opened fire on the demonstrators. Hundreds, perhaps even thousands, of demonstrators were killed. The incident, known as the Tiananmen Square Massacre, set off international protest, severely damaging China's reputation in the West.

In 1997, Tiananmen Square was the site of a massive celebration. Hong Kong, a port leased to the British for ninety-nine years after the defeat of the Qing army during the Opium Wars, was returned to China. As the British flag was lowered and the red flag of China was raised above Hong Kong, thousands gathered in Tiananmen Square to celebrate. Two years later, in 1999, Portugal returned the island of Macau to China.

One man blocks the way of tanks in the aftermath of the Tiananmen Square Massacre. He stopped their progress for half an hour.

Many have dubbed the twenty-first century "the pacific century." This name acknowledges China's military, technological, cultural, and economic might. China, the world's most populous nation, is poised to assume its role as the world's newest superpower.

Governing One Billion People

People jam the streets of Nanjing during a Chinese New Year celebration.

M ORE THAN A BILLION PEOPLE LIVE IN CHINA. Ruling a country so large is not easy. The most powerful institution in the nation is the Communist Party of China (CPC). The CPC sets goals and policy that the government then sets in motion.

The State Council

The State Council runs the government. The State Council is composed of a premier, vice premiers, state councilors, ministers in charge of departments and commissions, the auditor general, and the secretary general. The Central Committee of the Communist Party chooses the premier, China's head of government. The premier must be approved by the president, China's head of state, which is mainly a ceremonial job.

Opposite: **Beijing's Imperial Palace is the largest palace in the world.**

The State Council carries out the policies of the Communist Party. It also deals with China's internal politics, diplomacy, national defense, finance, economy, culture, and education.

The National People's Congress

China's legislative branch is the National People's Congress (NPC). Its 2,985 members serve five-year terms. The members of the NPC are chosen by the people's congresses in towns and provinces across China.

The main job of the NPC is to make laws, delegate authority, and supervise other government departments. According

Below right: **The National People's Congress, the home of China's legislature, appears on China's 100 yuan note.**

NATIONAL GOVERNMENT OF CHINA

Executive Branch

- STATE COUNCIL
- PREMIER
- VICE PREMIERS
- MINISTERS

Legislative Branch

- NATIONAL PEOPLE'S CONGRESS

Judicial Branch

- SUPREME PEOPLE'S COURT
- LOCAL PEOPLE'S COURT

中华人民共和国第十届全国人民代表大会第二次会议

to China's constitution, it is the highest government authority, but in fact it has little power.

The National People's Congress meets in a ten-thousand seat auditorium in the Great Hall of the People.

The Supreme People's Court

The Supreme People's Court is the highest court of law in China. The judges are appointed by the NPC. This court tries important cases and hears appeals related to the decisions of other courts. It supervises the work of local courts and special courts and can overrule their judgments. The Supreme People's Court also explains aspects of laws that must be carried out nationwide.

China's National Anthem

"The March of the Volunteers" was written in 1935 and adopted as China's national anthem in 1949, when the Communists gained control of the government. Tian Han wrote the words, and Nie Er composed the music.

Arise, ye who refuse to be slaves!
With our flesh and blood, let us build our new Great Wall!
The Chinese nation faces its greatest danger.
From each one the urgent call for action comes forth.
Arise! Arise! Arise!
Millions with but one heart,
Braving the enemy's fire.
March on!
Braving the enemy's fire.
March on! March on! March on!

The Military

The military in China is called the People's Liberation Army (PLA). During the Chinese Communist revolution, PLA members helped to recruit people to the Communist cause. For this reason, the PLA has played a major role in China's government since the establishment of the People's Republic of China in 1949.

Both men and women serve in the PLA, which currently includes 3 million troops. The minimum age for service is eighteen.

Members of the PLA are said to embody ideal Communist virtues: honesty, loyalty, bravery, selflessness, and initiative. On August 1 each year, the country honors the men and women in the military. Music ensembles of military units entertain millions of Chinese on television. They perform patriotic songs, folk songs, dances, and popular music. Life in the PLA is often the subject of popular daytime television dramas.

Justice

China's judicial system works to protect public property, maintain social order, guarantee smooth progress of the modernization drive, and punish criminals. People guilty of petty crimes, such as theft, might be sentenced to confess their

China's Flag

The national flag of the People's Republic of China has a bold red background and one large yellow star and four smaller yellow stars in the upper-left corner. The red background symbolizes revolution. The large star represents the Communist Party of China, and the four smaller stars represent the Chinese people.

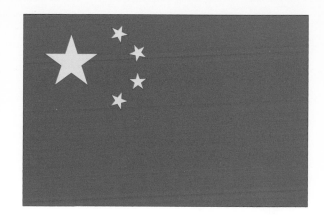

crime in front of their fellow workers. This public humiliation is supposed to prevent the behavior from being repeated. China also has a prison system. Some of these prisons require inmates to work in farming or manufacturing.

A criminal may be sentenced to death for a serious crime. In China, this includes not only violent acts, as in the West, but also crimes such as bribery or corruption. An example of this is the execution of a group of criminals who had manufactured a worthless medicine that looked like a real medicine. They sold the medicine for high prices. Those who needed the medicine suffered greatly, and some died. The criminals were sentenced to death and executed by firing squad. In China, death sentences are sometimes carried out in public or even broadcast on TV.

Guards bring prisoners out for public humiliation. Prisoners are often paraded in front of large crowds at rallies.

Beijing: Did You Know This?

Beijing straddles the traditional dividing line between Inner and Outer China. The name *Beijing* means "northern capital." The city was made the capital by the Mongols during the Yuan dynasty because it was midway between the traditional Mongolian homeland on the grasslands to the north and the center of Chinese agriculture to the south.

Beijing is China's second-largest city, with an estimated population of 7,441,000 people. The Old City, in the center of the capital, has many noted

palaces and temples. The most famous of these is the Forbidden City, the home of emperors beginning in the Ming dynasty. Work began on the Forbidden City in 1406. Today, it consists of eight hundred buildings and is the largest group of ancient wooden structures in the world. But much of Beijing is a modern, fast-paced city. It is filled with skyscrapers, and traffic jams are constant. This thriving, bustling city will host the Summer Olympics in 2008.

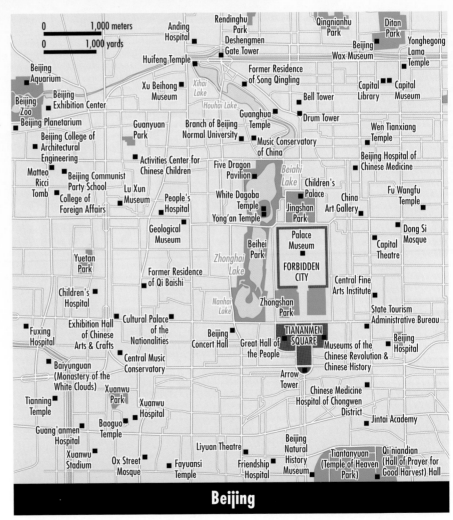

Beijing

The Sleeping Dragon Awakens

THE OPENING YEARS OF THE TWENTY-FIRST CENTURY HAVE seen China emerge as a major force in the international economic, cultural, and political arenas. Economists call it "the reawakening of the dragon."

Opposite: **More than two hundred thousand ships visit Hong Kong's harbor each year, making it one of the world's busiest ports.**

Feeding the Masses

Feeding the Chinese people without relying on other countries has been a top priority of the government since the founding of the People's Republic of China in 1949. Only 15 percent of Chinese territory is farmland, and much of it is vulnerable to flood and drought. The stability of the country rests on the government's ability to safeguard the livelihood of its people.

The Chinese often grow crops such as rice in steps cut into hillsides.

How can it feed a billion people? Today, China believes the answer lies in modernization. A series of flood-control projects is in the works. Irrigation channels are being built to expand farmland. And the nation's transportation network must be upgraded to carry products to wherever they are needed.

Prior to 1949, the country was devastated by war. Many irrigation systems broke down, and livestock populations dwindled. Agricultural output dropped drastically. Famine and disease were rampant. Mao Zedong carried out a series of reforms in rural areas. His most important program was land reform. Before land reform, tenant farmers were controlled by landlords. But throughout the 1950s, land was taken from the landlords and turned into communes, or collective farms. These communes were large farms run by the government.

Workers rake wheat on a commune in China.

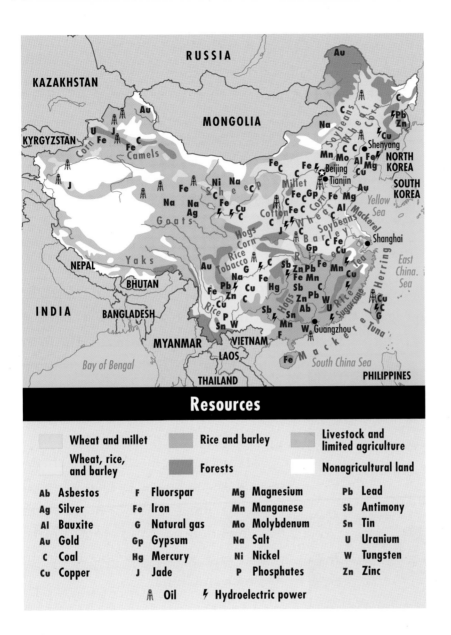

Resources

	Wheat and millet		Rice and barley		Livestock and limited agriculture
	Wheat, rice, and barley		Forests		Nonagricultural land

Ab	Asbestos	F	Fluorspar	Mg	Magnesium	Pb	Lead
Ag	Silver	Fe	Iron	Mn	Manganese	Sb	Antimony
Al	Bauxite	G	Natural gas	Mo	Molybdenum	Sn	Tin
Au	Gold	Gp	Gypsum	Na	Salt	U	Uranium
C	Coal	Hg	Mercury	Ni	Nickel	W	Tungsten
Cu	Copper	J	Jade	P	Phosphates	Zn	Zinc
		⚒	Oil	⚡	Hydroelectric power		

Deng Xiaoping, who took over after Mao's death, thought the country would grow more food without the communes. Although the land was still owned by the government, the decisions about what to grow on that land were left up to individual farmers. Agricultural output improved significantly.

Rice and Millet

In northern China, farmers cultivate millet and wheat on the plains and on the fertile loess plateau. To raise crops on the loess plateau, farmers developed terrace farming. In terrace farming, a series of steplike terraces are cut into the hillsides. The terraces wind around the hillsides to maximize the fertile areas.

In south China, rice is grown in well-watered river valleys. Rice paddies are dug into the earth and surrounded by low dikes that allow the farmers to flood the fields and drain them. Traditionally, men plow and irrigate the rice paddies, and women weed the crops.

Farmers harvest rice in Guizhou. Each year, China produces more than 140 million tons of rice.

Today, more than half of China's workers are farmers. China leads the world in the production of wheat, cotton, sweet potatoes, pears, and rice. In the north, wheat is the most common crop. In the south, the top crops are rice, sweet potatoes, and tea. Corn, sorghum, millet, peanuts, and carrots are also important crops.

Many farming families keep chickens, ducks, and hogs. In fact, China is home to about 350,000 hogs, about 40 percent of the world's total. Goats, cattle, and sheep are also common livestock in China.

Manufacturing

After the Communist Revolution, the government took over all industry. Economic and business decisions were made by the government. In the late 1950s, Chinese leaders began an all-out effort to establish industry. Much of the effort went into developing heavy industry, such as the manufacture of machinery and metals. Today, steel production is a leading industry in China. Cement, cars, trucks, ships, fertilizer, textiles, and electronics are other leading products.

The construction industry has also developed quickly. Offices and apartment buildings, highways, and airports have been built to meet the needs of China's huge population. Meanwhile, China's mining industry has grown. China is now the world's leading coal producer. It also has large reserves of petroleum and natural gas.

Workers build cars at a factory in Guangzhou. The number of cars produced in China has been growing steadily in recent years.

What China Grows, Makes, and Mines

Agriculture (2005)

Corn	130,000,000 metric tons
Rice	127,400,000 metric tons
Wheat	96,000,000 metric tons

Manufacturing

Cement (2003)	707,604,000 metric tons
Steel (2005)	345,000,000 metric tons
Automobiles (2003)	4,440,000 units

Mining (2003)

Coal	1,635,000,000 tons
Petroleum	3,392,000 barrels/day
Natural gas	35 billion cubic meters

Changing the Economy

Today, China's economic system is in transition. It is moving away from a centrally planned economy and toward a market economy. Agricultural communes were largely eliminated by 1984. Production decisions are now in the hands of the farmers. In industry, the decisions of local officials and plant managers have become more important than those of central planners. The government is also allowing the number of privately owned businesses to grow rapidly. Foreign technology and foreign investment are welcomed in China today.

China is now one of the world's leading traders. The government pumped money into state-owned businesses so that they could remain competitive with private companies and pay workers a living wage. These changes have resulted in a quadrupling

The production of electronics is one of China's many booming industries. About 22 percent of the Chinese labor force work in industry.

of the gross domestic product (GDP), or total value of goods and services produced by a country, since 1978.

Before 1978, workers in cities were assigned to jobs. People who worked for the government had fixed wages. Those who worked on collective farms or in factories were paid according to a system that did not reward how hard someone worked. The Chinese called this system the "iron rice bowl."

This began to change in 1978. That year, the rules were changed to allow bonus systems and rewards for the amount and difficulty of work done. In 1986, the State Council announced new regulations that made it possible to fire workers. This gave workers more incentive to do their jobs well. The reform of the labor system and the creation of a labor market have contributed to China's improved economy.

Pollution

In its race to industrialize, the Chinese government neglected to protect its water, air, and land against pollution. China is the world's second-largest producer of the dangerous greenhouse gases that harm the environment, trailing only the United States. In 2005, the Chinese government launched a program to clean up projects that are not in line with the country's environmental regulations. Huge construction projects were halted so that they could be brought up to standards.

At present, China relies on coal for most of its power. This is a problem, because coal produces a great deal of pollution. China is looking to develop clean, renewable energy sources, such as solar and wind power. In 2005, the government passed a law requiring power companies to use a certain amount of renewable power. This law should increase the use of renewable power sources to 10 percent of China's total consumption by 2020.

Currency

China's currency is called both Renminbi, which means "people's money," and yuan. The yuan is divided into ten jiao. Each jiao is made up of ten fen. Bills come in values of 1, 2, 5, 10, 20, 50, and 100 yuan and 1, 2, and 5 jiao. Coins are issued in 1, 2, and 5 fen. In 2005, 8.07 yuan equaled one U.S. dollar. Most paper money has a picture of Mao Zedong on the front and an image from nature on the back.

Hong Kong

The area known as Hong Kong consists of hundreds of islands and a small section of the mainland in southern China. During the Opium Wars of the nineteenth century, Great Britain forced China to lease Hong Kong. During the ninety-nine-year lease, Hong Kong thrived. It became a densely packed, bustling region and a center of international trade. In 1997, that lease finally ended. Hong Kong rejoined China.

Hong Kong is one of the most densely populated places in the world. In 2005, its many islands were home to nearly seven million people.

Although Hong Kong is again part of China, it has a high degree of self-rule. Its independence is based on an idea known as "one country, two systems." Under this system, Hong Kong's economic system has remained unchanged. It also has been free to maintain and develop relations with other countries.

Recently, however, a series of economic disasters hit Hong Kong. The first of these was the outbreak of a deadly bird flu. Construction on the Hong Kong International Airport has been dogged by mismanagement and has been a major headache for importers. More troubling is that the real estate and stock prices have suffered dramatic declines. Despite these setbacks, Hong Kong's economy remains strong.

Facing the Future

The Chinese economy is expected to grow at an annual rate of 8 percent from 2006 to 2010. China's continued rapid industrialization will strain its resources and environment even further. In addition, the nation will be under continued

China's Systems of Weights and Measures

The People's Republic of China uses the metric system for international trade. Within the nation, the Chinese weigh and measure quantities according to their traditional system. The chart below shows some Chinese weights and measures.

1 ch'ih	1.175 feet	0.36 meter
1 li	0.31 mile	0.50 kilometer
1 mu	0.16 acre	0.07 hectare
1 jin	1.10 pounds	0.50 kilogram

pressure to address the gaps between rural and urban areas and among different regions. China must address all of these challenges effectively in order to keep its economy vibrant and growing. The newly awakened dragon must be ever vigilant as it leads the world into the Pacific Century.

Though China has many bustling, modern cities, it is also home to hundreds of millions of people who live on farms and in small villages.

People of the People's Republic

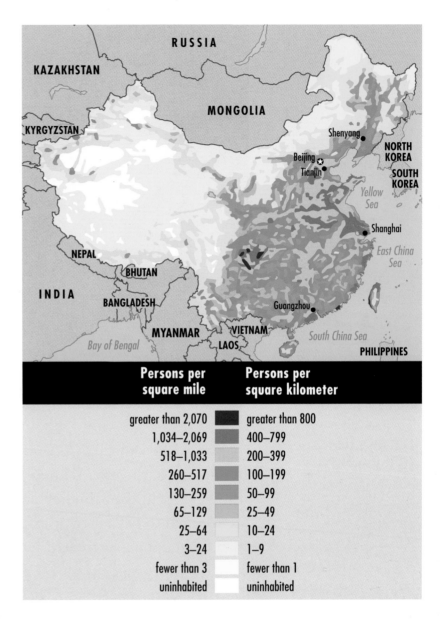

C HINA WAS THE first nation to have a population that topped a billion. In 2005, the country had an estimated 1,306,313,812 people— one-fifth of all the people on the face of the Earth.

At times in its history, China has suffered famine. In the 1970s, as the population was rapidly increasing, China moved to make sure it could feed everyone. In 1979, it began a policy of allowing couples to have only one child. The government could find no other way to slow the growth of the country's exploding population. Although people around the world complained that the rule was extreme and unfair, the policy has, in some ways, been effective. While China's population is still growing, that growth is at a much slower rate than it once was.

Opposite: **A girl from Tibet, one of the least densely populated parts of China**

It is estimated that China's one-child policy reduced the nation's population by 300 million in its first twenty years.

Holding Up Half the Sky

An old Chinese saying goes, "Women hold up half the sky." But in the twenty-first century, China's one-child policy and a traditional preference for male children has caused the Chinese population to become slanted in favor of males. There are about fifty-two males for every forty-eight females.

Today, the one-child policy is strictly enforced in cities. In rural areas, the rules tend to be more lax. Chinese couples who have additional children are subject to fines. Often, they are required to pay for their extra children's education rather than having the government provide schooling for free. This can be a heavy burden.

There are exceptions to China's one-child policy. For instance, the policy applies only to the Han, who make up about 92 percent of China's population. The Han are descendants of China's first great dynasty. They share the same cultural traditions, and most speak the same language, Mandarin Chinese. Members of minority groups, on the other hand, are allowed to have more than one child.

Digging Up the Past

The Chinese are building highways, airports, and houses at a rapid pace to meet the needs of their growing nation. Workers on these projects have sometimes stumbled across the glories of China's past. They have uncovered ancient burial sites, palaces, and towns.

The Chinese government tries to salvage these relics and preserve them for future generations. The Chinese approach to archaeology follows Communist ideas. Ancient sites are explored not just to show the glories of emperors, but also to celebrate the lives and accomplishments of the ordinary people of China.

One of the most spectacular finds in recent years was not an ancient relic but a person from the Han dynasty itself. A tomb in Hunan Province contained both the grave goods and the perfectly preserved body of the Lady of Dai. The woman died between 178 B.C. and 145 B.C. Her body had been enclosed in nested lacquer coffins and surrounded with charcoal and clay. These were ideal conditions for the body to be preserved. She still had blood in her veins and hair on her head, and her skin was still flexible.

After the Lady of Dai was discovered, doctors performed medical exams on her. They discovered that she had suffered from heart disease and that she had a bad back. They analyzed the contents of her stomach and found that her last meal was melon seeds.

Population of Major Cities (2003)

Shanghai	17,420,000
Beijing	14,230,000
Tianjin	10,113,000
Wuhan	7,565,000
Guangzhou	7,376,700

The government of the People's Republic of China recognizes fifty-five minority ethnic groups. These groups make up about 8 percent of China's population. Many minorities live in Outer China, especially the borderlands such as Tibet, Mongolia, Xinjiang, and Xishuangbanna.

Tibetans

Most of Tibet is an immense plateau at an altitude of 13,000 to 16,500 feet (4,000 to 5,000 m) above sea level. The majority of Tibet's 2 million people live in the valleys in the south.

Tibetans have their own language, religion, and literature. Tibetan history begins with invasions of the Tibetan army into neighboring regions in the seventh century. The Tibetans expanded their territory, controlling Nepal and parts of Yunnan Province as well as the famous Silk Routes, the caravan routes across northern China.

In the ninth century, Tibet broke up into feuding states. As the state lost control, the influence of the Buddhist clergy increased. Tibetan Buddhism adopted many of the customs of Bon, the traditional religion of the region, including flying prayer flags and turning prayer wheels. After the ninth century, the Buddhist monasteries became increasingly political. The lamas, or monks, were led by a spiritual ruler called the Dalai Lama, which means "teacher whose wisdom is great as the ocean."

Tibetans believe that each Dalai Lama is the reincarnation of the last, and that the spirit of one is present in the next. When a Dalai Lama dies, the monks search Tibet for the next

Dalai Lama. They look for a newborn child who shows some sign of the previous Dalai Lama's spirit.

In 1959, the present Dalai Lama fled to India after fighting broke out between Tibetans and the People's Liberation Army. More than 80,000 Tibetans fled to India and Nepal at that time. Although China took over Tibet in 1951, Tibet maintains some self-government.

The Dalai Lama is famous the world over. He received the Nobel Peace Prize in 1989 for his work encouraging Tibetans to resist the use of violence in their struggle for independence.

Mongolians have relied on horses since before the time of Genghis Khan. Even today, Mongolia has more horses than people.

Mongols

The traditional Mongol homeland lies along the banks of the Onon River, which now forms part of the border between China and the country of Mongolia. Here, in the vast grasslands beyond the Great Wall, the Mongols led a nomadic life, herding sheep and raising horses.

Today, the Mongols are scattered throughout China's northeastern provinces as well as through Qinghai and Xinjiang. About 2.8 million people live in Mongolia, which was once called Outer Mongolia. Inner Mongolia, which stretches across half of northern China, has almost 24 million people, including about 4 million Mongols. The Mongols are now a minority in their own traditional land.

The major Mongol festival is the annual Nadam Fair held during the summer months on the grasslands. Mongols, living in traditional yurts (tents) made of felt, flock to the festival. Here they compete in traditional Mongol sports, such as archery, wrestling, and horsemanship.

The Mongols were great horsemen and warriors. In 1206, the various factions of Mongols were united by Genghis Khan. In 1211, they began their conquest of the Chinese. The Yuan dynasty was founded in 1279 by Ghenghis's grandson, Kublai Khan. Descriptions of the fantastic Yuan capital in Beijing are found in stories told by Marco Polo, who may have never actually visited the capital. Eventually, the Mongols conquered lands beyond China. Their empire stretched from Burma to Russia—the largest empire in the history of the world.

Today, Inner Mongolia is governed by officials in Beijing. The Chinese language is compulsory in school, but Mongols also have their own written language. The Mongols are predominantly Buddhist, though some are Muslim.

Ethnic China

Han	92%
Other (55 ethnic groups, including Zhuang, Manchu, Hui, Uygur, Mongolian, and Tibetan)	8%

Above left: **Millions of Uygurs live in northwestern China.**

Above right: **The Uygurs are Muslim. Their ancestors converted to Islam between the 900s and the 1400s.**

Uygurs

Xinjiang is a region in western China that covers 17 percent of China's total land area. It is home to Han Chinese as well as thirteen of China's official fifty-five minority peoples, including Tajiks, Kergezs, Uzbeks, Kazakhs, and Uygurs.

The Uygurs, the largest minority group of the area, are Caucasians. They are larger and heavier than the Chinese, and their language is related to Turkish. Uygur women wear long skirts or dresses. Their heads are covered with brightly colored scarves or embroidered caps. The men wear embroidered caps and carry daggers. The Uygurs are Muslims. Their main food is lamb, barbecued over an open fire. They also raise grapes and melons. The Uygurs are famous for their music and graceful dancing.

The Dai

China's southernmost province, Yunnan, is home to many minority groups. Located in the deep south of Yunnan near the Laotian border is the region of Xishuangbanna. Here, in the tropical rain forest, live the Dai people. They were driven there by the Mongol invasion of China in the thirteenth century.

The Dai people build their wooden houses on stilts to keep them above the damp earth of the rain forest. Pigs and chickens live below the houses. The traditional Dai dress is a sarong—a large piece of fabric wrapped around the waist as a skirt—and a straw hat. The women have upswept hairstyles. The Dai are Buddhists. Their major holiday is the Water Splashing Festival held in April. The festival is held to wash away the sorrow and demons of the old year and bring happiness for the new.

Ethnic Groups

Dai	Miao-Yao	Tibeto-Burman
Han (Chinese)	Mongolian	Tungusic
Indonesian	Mon-Khmer	Turkic
Korean	Tajik	Uninhabited

Uniting all these different peoples under one flag has been a challenge for the People's Republic of China. To strengthen the bonds, the Chinese government has poured vast amounts of material and manpower into the regions where minority groups live. Many of these groups live in harsh conditions that make farming extremely difficult. The government supplies them with grain, fertilizer, and farming equipment.

The government has also built schools to raise the level of education and has attempted to train minority people as government officials. The hope is that this will help incorporate minority groups into the fabric of Chinese society.

Aging

Since the founding of the People's Republic of China in 1949, the average life expectancy of the Chinese has doubled. In old China, the average life span was thirty-four years; in 2000, it was seventy-one years. This improvement is due in large part to better health care.

The Confucianism of traditional China was centered on respect for elders, beginning with the respect of children for their parents. Respect for elders included the idea that children should care for their elderly parents and prepare lavish funerals for them.

Since the fall of Confucianism, along with the rise of individual freedom and China's one-child policy, many young Chinese feel that they are no longer responsible for the care of their aging parents. Today, many people expect the government to fill that role. The tradional Chinese family is changing quickly.

Language

All citizens of the People's Republic of China are taught Mandarin Chinese in school. Minority people may speak their own language in addition to Mandarin, and some Han speak other dialects of Chinese, such as Min or Wu. These dialects are so different that people speaking different dialects cannot understand each other.

Spoken Chinese relies on tones, or the way a word is spoken. Mandarin has four tones: high, rising, falling, and falling and then rising again. The meaning of the word changes depending on which tone is used. For example, *da* can mean either "to answer," "to hit," "big," or "to hang over something."

Common Mandarin Chinese words and phrases:

Ni hao (nee how)	Hello
Qing (cheeng)	Please
Xie xie (she-eh she-eh)	Thank you
Bu xie (buu she-eh)	You're welcome
Zai-jian (zigh-jee-in)	Good-bye
. . . *zai nar?* (zigh nah-urr)	Where is . . .?

People of the People's Republic **89**

Inventing Writing

Chinese legend tells about the invention of writing more than five thousand years ago by an official who worked for the emperor. The official devised a system of writing after being inspired by animal tracks. At this invention, says the legend, "all the spirits cried out in agony, as the innermost secrets of nature were revealed."

The Chinese originally used bamboo strips and silk for writing. During the Han dynasty, an official named Cai Lun invented paper made of bamboo, hemp, and mulberry bark.

Writing Chinese characters is the most respected art in China.

Written Chinese does not have an alphabet. Instead, it has characters that stand for a word or part of a word. Chinese has about fifty thousand characters, but only about four thousand of them are used in daily life.

Dragon Bones

In the 1800s, farmers in the Yellow River valley in northern China often found bones with strange carvings on them. The farmers called them "dragon bones" because they believed they came from the mythical creatures. The local Chinese believed these bones had special healing powers, and they were used to make traditional Chinese medicine.

Chinese scholars realized that the strange carvings were an ancient system of writing. Thousands of these bones were unearthed at Anyang. They date back to the Shang dynasty, about 1500 B.C. to 1046 B.C. Archaeologists called the writing *jia gu wen* (oracle-bone writing). About two thousand characters of this ancient written language have been recorded. Of these, about half have been deciphered. The carvings on these bones are questions from the Shang king to his ancestors regarding harvests, weather, hunting, and the birth of sons. Heated stalks of millet were put against the bones until the bones cracked. The king "read" the cracks to determine the spirits' answers.

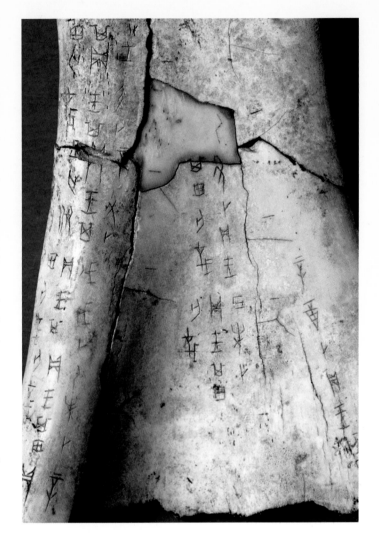

Since written Chinese has so many characters, for much of Chinese history, only those with a good education could read and write. After the Communists took over, they set out to teach every citizen of the People's Republic of China to read. They developed simplified versions of many characters.

During the Long March, each person had one important character written on the back of his or her jacket. The marchers were instructed to learn a new character each day by walking behind a different person. By the end of the Long March, each person knew several hundred Chinese characters. This was

About twenty thousand people survived the Long March. Many learned to read during the march, which lasted more than a year.

the foundation of literacy in modern China. Today, over 90 percent of Chinese age fifteen and over can read and write.

Chinese Names

Like most children in the West, the first thing a Chinese child learns to write is his or her name. A Chinese name begins with the family name. This reflects the importance of the family in traditional Chinese society. The individual is less important than belonging to a family. Some common family names in China are *Wang* (king), *Lee* (plum), *Zhang* (to draw a bow), and *Chen* (coin).

A person's family name is usually followed by two given names. In many cases, the first given name indicates a particular generation in that person's family. That character might come from a family poem. The second of the two given names often shows a special wish for the child. Boys' names might contain a reference to brilliance or luck, or they might signal a responsibility to the ancestors. For girls, a flower name is often given to signify beauty or a feminine trait.

The Chinese often use nicknames. Nicknames may be based on where the person was born, a particular physical trait, or an accomplishment.

Xingming

In Chinese, the word *xing* means "family name" and the word *ming* refers to a person's given names. When asking a person's name, the Chinese say, "Your honorable family name?" A request for a person's full name would be, "Your xing/ming?"

Between Heaven and Earth

CHINA IS OFFICIALLY AN ATHEIST STATE, MEANING THAT the government discourages the practice of any religion. The government sees religion as a potential threat. The Chinese Constitution does, however, claim to protect freedom of worship. Officially, it is estimated that 20 to 30 percent of the population engage in long-practiced religions such as Daoism, Buddhism, and Islam. Christians officially account for 2 to 3 percent of the population. But reliable information about religious practices in China is very hard to come by.

Opposite: **A giant statue of Buddha in Sichuan Province**

China has more than thirty-two thousand mosques.

Today, interest in religion is on the rise in China, but it is strictly controlled. Mosques, temples, and churches must be approved by the government. People are free to worship as they please, but preaching outside the walls of approved religious centers is forbidden.

Buddhism, Islam, Christianity, and Judaism all took root in China at one time or another. These, however, were seen as foreign religions or philosophies, unlike Confucianism and Daoism, which are native to China. The beliefs of many Chinese are a mixture of Confucianism, Buddhism, and Daoism.

Between Heaven and Earth **95**

Religion and the Cultural Revolution

During the Cultural Revolution, temples, mosques, and churches were destroyed. Buddhist, Muslim, and Christian leaders were not allowed to practice their religion. Instead, they were sent into the countryside to work on the land and be "reeducated" in Communist principles.

Although all religions and philosophies came under attack during the Cultural Revolution, the teachings of Confucius, with their important political message, were singled out. Confucianism was viewed as a symbol of the oppression of imperial China.

Confucianism

The principles of the ancient philosopher Confucius are a defining source of Chinese culture and thinking. The sayings of Confucius are recorded in *The Analects*. Confucian philosophy is not focused on an idea of heaven. Instead, it is firmly based on earthly life and the relationships between people. According to Confucius, one never acts alone. Instead, one's actions always affect others, and people must not create harm or tension. The correct way to rule, Confucius argued, is to set a moral example for the people to follow.

During the Han dynasty, Confucianism was adopted as the state philosophy. *The Analects* became the foundation for all education in China. Confucianism was also the basis for training government officials until the establishment of the Republic of China in 1912.

The Confucian ideas of obedience to parents and respect for elderly people and ritual were in direct conflict with Communist ideas. Nevertheless, Confucianism, with its emphasis on stability and respect for order and authority, has been used by the Communists as a tool to keep order.

Religions of China

No religion	57%
Traditional Chinese religions (Confucianism, Daoism)	20%
Atheism	8%
Christianity	2%
Islam	1%

Daoism

At the center of Daoist philosophy is the *dao*, or the "way." The dao is the ultimate reality and mystery of life. It is the driving force of nature and the idea behind the order of the universe. It can never be exhausted.

Daoists reject aggression, competition, and ambition. Humility and selflessness are thought to go hand in hand with the rejection of material goods, high rank, and social status. For Daoists, society is class-free and democratic. Because of this, Daoism is associated with political protest and rebellion.

Yin and Yang

Yin and yang is a concept in Chinese philosophy that consists of two opposing yet complementary forces. Yin is the female, passive, cool force. Yang is the male, active, hot force. These forces are engaged in an endless cycle of movement and change. This is best illustrated by the *taiji*, a symbol that shows a light patch and a dark patch winding around each other. This symbol shows how each of the two forces contains some of the opposing force. As yang reaches its peak, it changes into yin. As the cycle continues and yin peaks, it changes into yang. This never-ending cycle of peaks and valleys expresses the Chinese view of life, history, and everything else in the world. The concept of yin and yang probably goes back to an ancient religion, now lost. Yin and yang appear in Confucianism and are common in Daoism.

Buddhism

Buddhism is centered not on a god, but on attaining nirvana, a condition beyond the limits of the mind and body. The Buddhist religion began in India. A rich prince named Siddhartha became overwhelmed by a world filled with suffering. At the age of thirty, he gave up his worldly ties and began a search for enlightenment. He left his comfortable home, lived as a poor monk, and focused on meditation. While meditating, he came to the understanding that people could achieve nirvana by letting go of their worldly desires. Others began calling him Buddha, which means "the Enlightened One."

Carved Buddhas

Before Buddhism, the Chinese did not make sculptures that represented spiritual ideas. After Buddhism became prominent, a series of massive Buddhas began to appear on China's landscape. Some of the most famous of these carved Buddhas are in the caves at Longmen and Yungang. This colossal statue at Longmen (below) originally had a wooden framework to support a canopy above the Buddha's head.

At Dunhuang, along the Silk Routes, 492 caves carved into the cliffs and decorated with painted plaster have survived. Dunghuang became an important site for Buddhist pilgrims.

Chinese medicine is based on very different ideas from Western medicine. The idea behind Chinese medicine is that people live between heaven and earth and that each person makes up a miniature universe in himself. The material of which living things are made belongs to the yin. The life functions of living things belong to the yang. Finding the balance in the body's yin and yang is the guiding principle of traditional Chinese medicine.

The Chinese believe the body has five centers: the heart, lungs, liver, spleen, and kidneys. Changes in the seasons or weather can influence these centers. A person's living environment and personal relationships also affect these centers.

Chinese medicines are made from a mixture of plant parts.

原生草藥堂
祖传专配
肾虚腰痛 阳萎不举
阴虚阳虚 自汗盗汗
各类药酒 疑难杂症
特效追风膏

Medicinal herbs are sold in
markets across China.

Shen Nong, a legendary Chinese emperor who lived five thousand years ago, is considered the father of Chinese medicine. According to legend, Shen Nong tested hundreds of different plants to discover their nutritional and medicinal properties.

The Chinese prescribe a combination of herbs, brewed into a soup, to cure various illnesses. Peach pits and safflower, for example, are used to improve blood circulation. Ginseng is used to strengthen the heart. Cassia bark is used to treat colds.

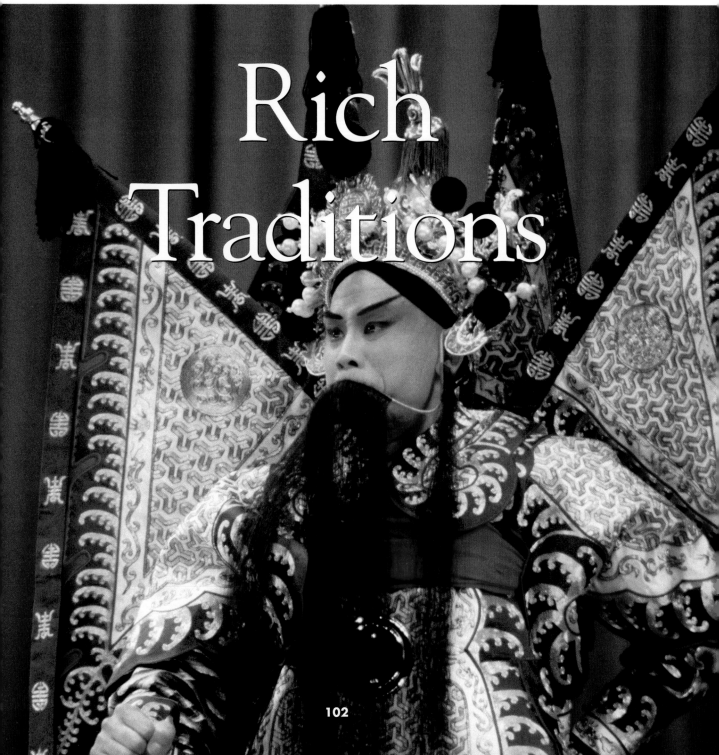

Rich
Traditions

CHINA HAS ANCIENT AND EXTRAORDINARY TRADITIONS in the arts. Some artists working today are continuing these traditions, while others are thoroughly modern and international.

Chinese Opera

Chinese opera is a special form of theater. It is one of China's most popular entertainments. It has been beloved by both young and old for centuries. Since imperial times, opera has often been found in the marketplace. For a few cents, shoppers can watch a performance while enjoying a snack and sipping tea.

The art of Chinese opera dates back to the 700s.

Masks

The facial makeup in Chinese opera tells the audience about the personality and intentions of the character. Red symbolizes loyalty and courage. People wearing black makeup are adventurous. Characters wearing white makeup cannot be trusted. Their trickery will have an important role in the plot. The makeup in Chinese opera is elaborate. It sometimes takes many hours to apply it.

Zhang Yimou's films are famous for their rich color and visual style. He has received two Academy Award nominations for best foreign film.

Operas are often based on historical events. Stylized gestures, gymnastics, and elaborate makeup and costumes are all part of the performance. Opera performers begin training when they are very young in order to learn the necessary singing skills, eye movements, gestures, and gymnastics. They spend years practicing their skills.

Film

Zhang Yimou is a member of China's famous Fifth Generation film directors. This innovative group came of age during the Cultural Revolution and worked to establish a contemporary style of Chinese film.

Zhang's films are noted for their use of the color red, particularly in such films as

Raise the Red Lantern and *Red Sorghum*. Although Zhang has been celebrated around the world, he has been criticized in his own country by people who claim that his films promote Western stereotypes of China. Zhang has often collaborated with the actress Gong Li. She is China's best-known actress in the West.

Gong Li appeared in seven of Zhang Yimou's films. No other Chinese actress is as well known in the West.

The Three Perfections

The arts of calligraphy, poetry, and painting are called the "Three Perfections" in China. Since the Song dynasty (960–1279), the practice of the Three Perfections has been viewed as the mark of an educated person. All educated men and women take part in this artistic tradition. As a result, more people practice these arts in China than in the West. The Chinese feel that the combination of calligraphy, poetry, and painting is the height of artistic expression. The Chinese often combine the three in a single work.

Chinese paintings often include calligraphy and poetry.

Painting

Chinese art tends to be concerned with nature and the workings of the universe. Western art, on the other hand, tends to be more concerned with the human body and human emotions. The Chinese feel that human life is just a small part of the universe.

The Chinese view the universe as composed of two forces—yin and yang. Yin, the female force, is cool and passive. It is best represented by water. Yang, the male force, is hot and active. It is best represented by rocks and mountains. By painting a landscape composed of these two elements, the Chinese portray a universe that is both in balance and continually changing. So a landscape painting for the Chinese is not just a picture of scenery, but a statement about a world where all elements are in balance.

Traditionally, Chinese paintings have included writing, or inscriptions. For example, one scholar might paint a landscape. Another would write a line of poetry on the painting. A third might add an inscription describing the circumstances under which the work was done. Over the years, other scholars would add comments of appreciation for the work. The Chinese felt that viewing such a work and adding a fresh inscription allowed

The Chinese term for landscape is shansui, which means "mountains and water." These two elements represent yin and yang in the universe.

scholars to connect over the years and miles that separated them. This allowed a painting to grow.

In Communist China, calligraphy by famous politicians was sometimes added to a painting. Mao's calligraphy appears on a landscape of rivers and mountains. In Western art, no one would ever write on another person's painting. It would be considered vandalism. But this practice is highly respected in China.

In contemporary China, artists have used Western techniques and ideas to expand their approach to art. Nevertheless, the traditional combination of image and word is still a common way that artists express themselves.

The international flavor of contemporary art crosses all cultural and political boundaries. But many of today's Chinese artists depend on a link with China's past, especially politics and calligraphy, to produce their art. Chinese artist Cai Guoqiang uses fireworks, which were invented in China, as art. In one project that reflected on China's relationship with the world, he used fireworks to both extend the Great Wall and make it seem to disappear.

Calligraphy

For the Chinese, writing is a way of communicating many things. Chinese people don't just read the words, they look at the way the words are written. They believe that a person's handwriting is like a fingerprint of his or her thoughts.

This attitude toward handwriting developed with the invention of paper during the Han dynasty. With paper, the reader could see every movement of the hand that wrote the complex Chinese characters. Nothing could be hidden, erased, or corrected. Likewise, the Chinese felt that writing revealed a person's inner character. For these reasons, the Chinese considered calligraphy to be the highest art form. A bold and balanced handwriting meant the person was courageous and moderate. Sloppy, weak characters indicated a lazy mind that was not dependable.

Language is the focus of the work of the contemporary artist Xu Bing. In one case, Xu printed thousands of nonsensical Chinese-style characters of his own invention. The printed pages were arranged on the wall, on banners hanging from the ceiling, and in books on the floor. The work's strange Chinese characters both invite and frustrate the reader, bringing to mind books from China's imperial age to the present.

Calligrapher Liu Zhou Zhou works in his studio.

Music

Music is the most ancient of the arts. The Chinese believe it has the power to transform and elevate people's minds. Composer and conductor Tan Dun breaks the boundaries between East and West. His music mixes ancient Chinese music and modern experimentation. In his Water Concerto, he uses water in bottles, tubes, and bowls as musical instruments. His operas often draw on Chinese traditional texts. They include *Tea: A Mirror of the Soul*, *Peony Pavilion*, and *Marco Polo*. Tan Dun also wrote the Oscar Award–winning original score for the mystical martial-arts film *Crouching Tiger, Hidden Dragon*.

Lang Lang began playing piano at age three. He won his first competition at age five.

Lang Lang, who was born in 1982 in Shenyang, is one of the most celebrated pianists in the world. Lang Lang studied piano at both the Central Music Conservatory in Beijing and the Curtis Institute in Philadelphia. When Lang Lang made his Carnegie Hall recital debut in 2001, he was just nineteen years old. That night, the audience was treated to a special performance joining the music of East and West. The pianist called his father, a master of the erhu, a Chinese string instrument, to the stage. The two performed a Chinese classical duet, earning enthusiastic applause from the audience.

Night Thoughts

Many of China's greatest poets lived during the Tang dynasty (618–907). One of these poets, Li Po, lived from 701 to 762. His poems are famous for their humor and emotions as well as for their descriptions of dreams and nature. This poem is called "Night Thoughts":

The bright moon shone
before my bed,
I wondered—
was it frost upon the ground?
I raised my head
to gaze at the clear moon,
Bowed my head
remembering my old home.

Poetry

China has a rich literary history. *The Book of Songs* is one of the earliest known examples of Chinese literature. It is a collection of three hundred poems that dates back three thousand years. These poems concern subjects such as love, war, and farming. Chinese poetry relies on the unique character of the Chinese language. Since the Chinese language has a variety of tones, Chinese poems need to be balanced in tone as well as in rhythm and rhyme.

Sports

Some sports that are popular in China are common around the world. Soccer, the most popular sport in the world, is tremendously popular in China. But Ping-Pong is equally popular. Chinese kids follow Ping-Pong with the same enthusiasm that American kids follow basketball or baseball. Chinese players usually dominate the Ping-Pong competition at the Olympics.

Chinese athletes stunned the world with their performances at the 2004 Olympics in Greece. China ranked second after the United States in the number of medals, with thirty-two gold, seventeen silver, and fourteen bronze medals. Chinese athletes even took medals in track and field and other sports in which they do not traditionally do well. In 2008, the world comes to Beijing for the Summer Olympics.

Chinese women won the gold medal in volleyball at the 2004 Olympics in Athens, Greece.

People flying kites atop the Great Wall. Kites were invented more than three thousand years ago in China.

Games

Kites, tops, and yo-yos are popular toys with children around the world. All three have their roots in China.

Kites made of silk or paper stretched across a bamboo frame were first made in China. Kites were tools in China before they were toys. The ancient Chinese used silk kites to communicate with heavenly spirits. They wrote messages asking for rain or good harvests on the kites and then released the kites to carry their messages to the heavens.

The Chinese realized that kites could be used for military purposes, such as calling troops to action. By constructing huge kites in the form of eagles, the Chinese flew men above enemy troops to report on their movements. Today, this military history of kites is reflected in the Chinese sport of kite fighting. Competitors cover the line nearest the kite with

Kite making is sometimes an art form in China. Here, Liu Han Xiang shows off one of his masterpieces.

ground glass or sand. Using the lines as saws, they try to cut their opponent's kite loose by engaging in a series of swoops, dodges, and darts.

When the Chinese invented paper during the Han dynasty (206 B.C.–A.D. 220), kite flying became an inexpensive amusement for everyone. It also became part of folk festivals. Today, the skies over China are often filled with colorful kites. The Chinese call kites *feng zhen* ("wind zither") because of the sound the wind makes as it passes through holes in the kite's bamboo frame.

Tops have been found at prehistoric burial sites in China. A top may be made of bamboo, seedpods, acorns, or shells, depending on the environment of the region.

A double top, which spins along a string stretched between two poles, is called a diablo in the west. This top can be flipped in the air and caught on the string. Another kind of Chinese spinning toy is made of two disks of wood that travel up and down a string. In 1932, the Duncan Toy Company copyrighted the name *yo-yo* and popularized the toy in the West.

Uygur boys playing with tops. Tops dating back to 1250 B.C. have been found in China.

Once paper became inexpensive, the Chinese manufactured a number of games made of paper. A folded paper toy is used in POGS, a game recently introduced in North America. In the Chinese version of POGS, the paper is folded into triangles. Each player tries to whip his own POG over the other players' pieces.

The number-one hobby in today's China is stamp collecting. Both adults and children eagerly collect postage stamps from around the world. China's own postage stamps often feature scenic spots in China or historic events in the People's Republic of China.

Gongfu takes great self-discipline and motivation.

Gongfu

Perhaps the sport that Westerners most associate with the Chinese is *gongfu* (kung fu), a term that has entered the English language thanks to the late martial-arts star Bruce Lee. Today, gongfu includes boxing, weapon wielding, and different types of exercises used to promote good health. Some types of gongfu exercise the body's tendons, bones, and skin. Many of these exercises are based on the movements

The feats of Chinese acrobats amaze fans around the world.

of animals, such as the tiger, panther, monkey, snake, and crane. Other gongfu trains the spirit and the mind. Each day, as dawn breaks, the streets begin to fill with Chinese gathering to perform the traditional exercises.

Acrobatics

Balance, strength, flexibility, and grace are all found in Chinese acrobatics. Acrobatics include balancing and tumbling as well as juggling swords, balls, and pottery containers. The acrobatic troupe from Shanghai has toured the world to great acclaim, acting as China's cultural ambassador.

Life in China

FOR THOUSANDS OF YEARS, CHINESE FARMERS HAVE AWAKened at dawn in order to start their day before the sun makes work too difficult. Today, about half the people in China are still engaged in farming, and the dawn still signals the start of China's day.

People eat breakfast before setting out for work or school. In the north, breakfast usually includes noodles or bread made of wheat flour. Southern children often eat a rice porridge called *congee*, topped with shrimp, vegetables, or pickles. They might also enjoy a glass of soy milk, hot or cold, to which either sugar or soy sauce has been added.

Opposite: **Fishers on the Li River at sunrise**

Most rural Chinese rise at dawn, eat breakfast, and head out to work.

Oil Stick and Sesame Bread

Many street vendors in China sell a favorite breakfast treat: a fried bread sandwich. A soft-baked roll topped with sesame seeds is used to hold a piece of deep-fried dough called an oil stick.

The Chinese use chopsticks and a spoon to eat their meals. The Western custom of using a knife at the table is looked down upon. Chinese feel that knives should be used in the kitchen, but not at the table.

Chinese cooking methods show how a cook can make the most of the flavors of the ingredients using a minimum of fuel. Foods are chopped into small pieces and cooked quickly. The Chinese often stir-fry their foods in a pan called a wok. The cook coats the wok with a little oil and then moves the food around quickly in the pan.

A man cooks in woks at an outdoor market.

The Story of Tea

The origin of tea drinking in China is drenched in ancient legends. One legend tells that tea was discovered by a poor woodcutter who was in the hills one day when he noticed monkeys plucking and chewing the leaves of a particular tree. He tasted the leaves himself and found the taste soothing and refreshing. Soon, all his fellow villagers were using the leaves in drinks. Another legend ties the beverage to a king who was sitting under a tree when leaves fell into the pot of water he was boiling. He drank the water and found it delightful. Whatever the true origin of tea, throughout Chinese history, everyone—from farmers to emperors—has enjoyed the drink.

The Buddhist monk Lu Yu, who lived during the Tang dynasty (618–907), wrote the *Tea Classic*. He promoted tea as a drink to help monks stay alert during meditation. Lu organized the planting of tea trees around Buddhist monasteries. The popularity of tea spread with Buddhism across Asia.

Different kinds of tea are the result of different methods of processing the leaves. Various tastes, colors, and fragrances depend on the way the leaves are fermented and roasted. Today, there are hundreds of varieties of Chinese tea. These can be mainly classified into five categories: green tea, black tea, brick tea, scented tea, and oolong. Tea that has not been fermented is called green tea. This is the tea most Chinese drink. Foreigners are most likely to drink black tea. The Chinese would never add sugar, honey, lemon, or milk to their tea the way Westerners do.

The Chinese believe that tea improves eyesight and increases alertness. They consider tea to be a natural health food. Recently, Western scientists have discovered how green tea helps to prevent certain types of cancer.

Steamed dumplings are a popular food in China. Dumplings are stuffed with meat, seafood, or vegetables.

Steaming is another popular Chinese cooking method. To steam, the Chinese use flat-bottomed bamboo baskets that can be stacked on top of one another. Each basket is lined with a cabbage leaf. The food is placed inside the baskets, and then the stacked baskets are placed over a pan of boiling water. The steam from the water cooks the food.

Education

Chinese children begin attending school at age six or seven, and they must go for at least nine years. School is held six days a week. Since most families have only one child, children are under much pressure to succeed in school. High-school students preparing for college entrance exams face the greatest pressure. They study long and hard for these exams, because the tests determine what kind of school they can go to. Those who do the best go to a public university, where most study languages, math, a science, or economics. Students who do not do as well on the exams might go to a technical college, where they study such subjects as agriculture, medicine, or teaching.

Beijing University is the most prestigious school in China. Nearly thirty-seven thousand students attend the university.

Young Pioneers

The goal of every child is to do well in school and be recommended for the Young Pioneers. Young Pioneers are something like Boy Scouts and Girl Scouts. They are encouraged to develop self-reliance.

In China, Young Pioneers represent the ideal Communist traits of bravery, initiative, and self-sacrifice. Children in the Young Pioneers wear red neckerchiefs to symbolize the Communist future of their country. They often represent their class at school ceremonies.

A Child's Life

In China, the school day begins at 8:30 A.M. The first activity is ten minutes of exercises. After exercises, classes begin. The classes tend to be large. Children study subjects such as the Chinese language, history, music, math, science, and painting.

At noon, it's time for lunch. This is followed by a rest from one to two o'clock. Free time in the schoolyard is a favorite time for Chinese children, just as it is for children around the world. Many of the games played by Chinese children are familiar to children in the West. Others are Chinese games that date back thousands of years.

Jianzi is a sport similar to badminton, but it uses no racquets. In jianzi, children try to keep a shuttlecock in the air by catching it on the sole or heel of the foot. Chinese children often make their own shuttlecock by wrapping a bit of rag or soft leather around a coin with a hole in the middle. Goose quills are poked through the central hole to help keep the shuttlecock in the air.

Most students in Hong Kong wear uniforms. Elementary school students study both Chinese and English.

School ends at 4:30 P.M. After that, many children head to an after-school program. There they sing and dance, do artwork, or play games until their parents' workday is finished. On the way home, many children chat on their cell phones. It is estimated that by 2008, there will be 500,000,000 cell phones in China.

When the family meets for dinner, parents and children are often joined by grandparents, cousins, aunts, and uncles. Dinner, homework, perhaps checking the Internet, and then bed are the usual order of the evening. By 9 P.M., most parents and children are in bed, in anticipation of getting up early again the next day.

All Chinese children know that they are the new generation of the world's oldest continuous civilization. But they also understand that they are citizens of the world's most populous nation and an emerging superpower.

National Holidays in the People's Republic of China

New Year's Day	January 1
Spring Festival (Chinese New Year)	Date varies
International Working Women's Day	March 8
International Labor Day	May 1
Youth Day	May 4
Children's Day	June 1
Founding of the Communist Party of China Day	July 1
Founding of the People's Liberation Army Day	August 1
Teachers' Day	September 10
National Day	October 1–2

Timeline

China's History

The Yangshao culture reaches its peak in northern China.	**c. 3000** B.C.
The Shang dynasty develops.	**1700s** B.C.
The Zhou dynasty rules China.	**1045–256** B.C.
The great Chinese philosopher Confucius dies.	**479** B.C.
China is united as an empire under the Qin dynasty; construction begins on the Great Wall.	**221** B.C.
The Han dynasty rules China.	**206** B.C.–A.D. **220**
China breaks into smaller kingdoms.	**220**
The Sui dynasty reunites China.	**581**
Arts flourish under the Tang dynasty.	**618–907**
The Song dynasty takes control of China.	**960**
Mongol leader Kublai Khan defeats the Song and establishes the Yuan dynasty.	**1279**
The Ming overthrow the Mongols and establish their own dynasty.	**1368**
The Manchu overthrow the Ming and rule China as the Qing dynasty.	**1644**

World History

2500 B.C.	Egyptians build the Pyramids and the Sphinx in Giza.
563 B.C.	The Buddha is born in India.
A.D. **313**	The Roman emperor Constantine recognizes Christianity.
610	The Prophet Muhammad begins preaching a new religion called Islam.
1054	The Eastern (Orthodox) and Western (Roman) Catholic Churches break apart.
1066	William the Conqueror defeats the English in the Battle of Hastings.
1095	Pope Urban II proclaims the First Crusade.
1215	King John seals the Magna Carta.
1300s	The Renaissance begins in Italy.
1347	The Black Death sweeps through Europe.
1453	Ottoman Turks capture Constantinople, conquering the Byzantine Empire.
1492	Columbus arrives in North America.
1500s	The Reformation leads to the birth of Protestantism.
1776	The Declaration of Independence is signed.

China's History

The first Opium War begins.	1839
The Treaty of Nanjing gives Hong Kong to Britain.	1842
Westerners and Chinese Christians are massacred during the Boxer Rebellion.	1900
Chinese revolutionaries overthrow the Qing dynasty.	1911
Sun Yat-sen becomes president of the Chinese Republic.	1912
The Chinese Communist Party is founded.	1921
Chinese Nationalists and Communists fight a civil war.	1946–1949
Communist leader Mao Zedong declares the formation of the People's Republic of China; Chiang Kai-shek's Nationalist forces retreat to Taiwan and set up the Republic of China.	1949
The Cultural Revolution begins.	1966
The People's Republic of China is admitted to the United Nations.	1971
Mao Zedong dies.	1976
The army opens fire on students protesting government corruption in Beijing's Tiananmen Square.	1989
Great Britain returns control of Hong Kong to China.	1997
Portugal returns control of Macau to China.	1999
China's first manned spacecraft is launched; the Three Gorges Dam begins to generate electricity.	2003

World History

1789	The French Revolution begins.
1865	The American Civil War ends.
1914	World War I breaks out.
1917	The Bolshevik Revolution brings communism to Russia.
1929	Worldwide economic depression begins.
1939	World War II begins, following the German invasion of Poland.
1945	World War II ends.
1957	The Vietnam War starts.
1969	Humans land on the moon.
1975	The Vietnam War ends.
1979	Soviet Union invades Afghanistan.
1983	Drought and famine in Africa.
1989	The Berlin Wall is torn down as communism crumbles in Eastern Europe.
1991	Soviet Union breaks into separate states.
1992	Bill Clinton is elected U.S. president.
2000	George W. Bush is elected U.S. president.
2001	Terrorists attack World Trade Center, New York, and the Pentagon, Washington, D.C.

Fast Facts

Official name: People's Republic of China

Capital: Beijing

Official language: Mandarin Chinese

Beijing

People's Republic of China's flag

Chinese mountains

Official religion:	None
National anthem:	"The March of the Volunteers"
Government:	Single-party Communist government
Chief of state:	President
Head of government:	Premier
Area:	3,705,820 square miles (9,598,032 sq km)
Bordering countries:	Russia to the north; Kazakhstan, Kyrgyzstan, Tajikistan, Afghanistan, and Pakistan to the west; India, Nepal, Bhutan, Myanmar (Burma), Laos, and Vietnam to the south; and North Korea to the east
Highest elevation:	Mount Everest (Qomolangma), 29,028 feet (8,848 m)
Lowest elevation:	Turpan Depression in Xinjiang, 505 feet (154 m) below sea level
Average annual rainfall:	Northern deserts, less than 4 inches (10 cm); southeastern coast, 60–80 inches (150–200 cm)
National population (2005 est.):	1,303,306,812

Population of largest cities (2003):

Shanghai	17,420,000
Beijing	14,230,000
Tianjin	10,113,000
Wuhan	7,565,000
Guangzhou	7,376,700

The Great Wall

Currency

Famous landmarks: ▶ *The Great Wall*, northern China

▶ *Forbidden City*, Beijing

▶ *Lishan Mausoleum*, Shaanxi Province

▶ *Three Gorges,* Sichuan-Hubei border

▶ *Stone Forest*, Yunnan Province

▶ *Big Goose Pagoda*, Xian, Shaanxi Province

Industry: China's major industries are the manufacture of machinery, transportation equipment, and steel. Producing chemicals such as plastics and medicines is the country's second-largest industry. Textiles, food processing, and clothing are also important. Although light industry that produces consumer goods is growing, heavy industry still leads China's manufactured goods.

Currency: The Renminbi ("people's money"), also called the yuan. In 2006, one U.S. dollar equaled 8.05 yuan.

Weights and measures: China uses the metric system for international trade and a Chinese system within the nation.

Literacy rate: 90 percent

Schoolchildren

Gong Li

Common Mandarin Chinese words and phrases:

Ni hao (nee how)	Hello
Qing (cheeng)	Please
Xie xie (she-eh she-eh)	Thank-you
Bu xie (buu she-eh)	You're welcome
Zai-jian (zigh-jee-in)	Good-bye
. . . *zai nar?* (zigh nah-urr)	Where is . . . ?

Famous Chinese:

Cai Guoqiang   (1957–)
Artist

Deng Xiaoping   (1904–1997)
Communist leader

Gong Li   (1965–)
Actress

Lang Lang   (1982–)
Musician

Li Po   (701–762)
Poet

Mao Zedong   (1893–1976)
Communist leader

Tan Dun   (1957–)
Composer/conductor

Xu Bing   (1955–)
Artist

Zhang Yimou   (1950–)
Filmmaker

To Find Out More

Nonfiction

▶ Bowden, Rob. *Yangtze*. Chicago: Raintree, 2004.

▶ Dramer, Kim. *The Yellow River*. New York: Franklin Watts, 2001.

▶ Hatt, Christine. *Mao Zedong*. Milwaukee, Wis.: World Almanac Library, 2004.

▶ Locricchio, Matthew. *The Cooking of China*. New York: Benchmark, 2003.

Web Sites

▶ **Asian Art**
http://www.asianart.org
Information from the Asian Art Museum of San Francisco, one of the largest museums in the Western world dedicated exclusively to Asian art.

▶ **Asia Society**
http://www.asiasociety.org
Learn more about China from this institution, which is devoted to improving understanding between Asians and Americans.

▶ **Ask Asia**
http://www.askasia.org
For a variety of cultural information, engaging games and activities, and links to people, places, and institutions.

▶ **Chinese Culture**
http://www.chinaculture.org
For information on travel, culture, and archaeological finds from the Ministry of Culture of the People's Republic of China.

▶ **Chinese Current Events**
http://www.xinhuanet.com
For news updates from the official news service of the People's Republic of China.

Organizations and Embassies

▶ **Consulate-General of the People's Republic of China in New York**
520 12th Avenue
New York, NY 10036
212-868-7752

▶ **Embassy of the People's Republic of China**
2201 Wisconsin Avenue, NW
Washington, DC 20007
202-338-6688

Index

Page numbers in *italics* indicate illustrations.

Meet the Author

K IM DRAMER received her PhD from the Department of Art History and Archaeology of Columbia University. Her specialty is the art and archaeology of ancient China.

Writing this book for the Enchantment of the World series, she used the libraries at Columbia University, including the C.V. Starr East Asian Library. This is one of the finest collections of scholarly books on China in the world. She also relied on her own personal trips to China, where she has traveled extensively, including a trip across the Gobi Desert along the ancient Silk Routes. She is pictured (opposite) in front of the Big Goose Pagoda in Xian, an ancient capital of China.

Kim is the mother of twins, Alexandra and Max Wang. In Chinese, their names are Wang Xianhan and Wang Xiantang. They are named after the Han and Tang dynasties, two of China's most powerful and creative periods. Their grandfather John S. T. Wang, a noted calligrapher, provided the Chinese calligraphy that appears on page 10 of this book.

Photo Credits